Death Takes a HOLIDAY

Music and Lyrics by Maury Yeston

Jill Paice (Grazia) and Kevin Earley (Prince Sirki)
"Alone Here with You"

Photography by Joan Marcus

Piano/vocal arrangements by Maury Yeston

Cherry Lane Music Company
Director of Publications/Project Supervisor: Mark Phillips

ISBN 978-1-60378-420-7

Visit our website at www.cherrylaneprint.com

Jill Paice (Grazia)
"Finale"

THE POET LAUREATE OF LONGING

by Patrick Pacheco

Death had me at hello.

Not at "hello" exactly. This incarnate manifestation of that which all humans fear actually seduced me within the first few bars of the twin songs "Centuries" and "Why Do All Men?," his haunting and lyrical introduction in the new musical *Death Takes a Holiday.* And why not? After all, if anyone can make the Grim Reaper sing, it is Maury Yeston. And not just sing but yearn to know life and love itself:

"To breath a sigh…
If I could learn what words like hope and love
 and kindness truly are made of…
If I could learn what it may be to cry…
That would be a lesson worthy
Of this one-time-only journey…"

Teach Death…to cry? To learn pity and, in turn, to be pitied? What an extraordinary mandate. And yet what a natural progression for a composer who has never flinched from daunting challenges, whether it be discovering the beating heart within a disfigured freak *(Phantom),* mining the psychological complexities of a priapic artistic genius *(Nine),* juggling the romantic follies of a disparate group of adventurers *(Grand Hotel)* or celebrating the exalted dreams aboard a doomed ocean liner *(Titanic).*

Thus, after *Titanic* in 1997, Yeston and the librettist Peter Stone were irresistibly drawn to re-collaborate on a musical adaptation of Alberto Casella's 1924 play *La Morte in Vacanze,* which a decade later was made into the classic film *Death Takes a Holiday.* After the brutal and senseless carnage of World War I, Casella's fanciful conceit was that Death sorely needed a vacation. No fool, he assumes the royal personage of a handsome Russian prince and insinuates himself for a weekend into the villa of a wealthy Italian duke, Vittorio Lamberti. But what makes this vintage Yeston territory is the reason why Death stays his hand and decides to become human:

"Eons I've performed my duties
I've encountered greater beauties
What restrains me now, I wonder
Feeling her heart race?
Stops my instinct
To enfold her,
In the Great War
Not one solider
Fell to me with quite the pow'r
Of life within this face."

The intense longing expressed in the music is sufficient unto the cause—even as the minor chord on "face" fills us with a foreboding—because it is a woman who inspires Death to lay down his burden. The glimpse of Grazia, the lovely and graceful daughter of the Duke, is enough to stop Death in his tracks and to inspire the melancholy and yearning that is woven, like a golden thread, through all of Yeston's work. Diverse though it is, his music reaches its most profound height in what has long been the central preoccupation of the Broadway musical: "To connect, only connect," as the writer E. M. Forster succinctly put it. And *Death Takes a Holiday* adds a compelling and innovative chapter to Yeston's lifelong romantic obsession. For one, Grazia, though already engaged to another,

(left to right) Mara Davi (Alice), Rebecca Luker (Duchess Stephanie), Jay Jaski (Lorenzo), Jill Paice (Grazia), Max von Essen (Corrado), Michael Siberry (Duke Vittorio), and Alexandra Socha (Daisy)
"In the Middle of Your Life/Nothing Happened"

is primed for this sudden and transformative encounter with the mysterious stranger. For another, Death, as Prince Sirki, is charming, sophisticated, sexy, and…naïve. As naïve, in fact, as a newborn babe.

Which, of course, he is. Here is where Yeston and his collaborators have fun, in their typical fashion, turning the boy-meets-girl convention on its head. On his first morning, can Prince Sirki ever get enough of everything he lays eyes on, including the fried eggs brought in by the butler, the fresh towels brought in by the saucy maid, or the fragrances wafting through the windows out of which stretches the gorgeous Italian countryside?

"Not a moment more to waste
I can breathlessly begin to taste
Every sight and sound and smell
That may soon arrive…
Starting with the sunlight streaming
And warming up my skin, and beaming
Within me this new glow
Of coming alive!"

In this, Sirki resembles no one in dramatic literature more than Emily in *Our Town,* brought back to life for one day by the Stage Manager. "I can't stare at things hard enough," she says, exulting in the quotidian beauty of life. It takes a poet as sensitive as Yeston to capture that in "Life's a Joy," a song sung by the Lamberti household on that first bright morning. But the stakes are driven even higher with the first stirrings of the heart which, in a wry role-reversal, belong here to the man, not the woman. Forget the eggs. What really captures the virginal Sirki's attention is the come-hither stare of the maid, the shimmy taught to him by the sexy American widow staying at the villa, and the overpowering sensation and all-enveloping glow of first love.

The passionate romance between Prince Sirki and Grazia at the center of *Death Takes a Holiday* recalls a purer time in the American musical theater, a legacy of romance treated without cynicism and without apology that can be traced from *The Student Prince* to *Show Boat* to *West Side Story* to *Death Takes a Holiday.* In the song "Alone Here with You," which ends the first act, a pair of lovers, bathed in moonlight, sing their hearts out to each other. What could be more classic than that, and yet the moment is far from dated. In fact, it rings true, fresh and contemporary, made all the more so by its rarity in a theatrical landscape increasingly dominated by self-referential irony, satire, and lavish spectacle.

What lends the musical a special poignancy is the lucidity with which it demonstrates just how fast—and cruelly—love, friendship, and family can disappear. The long and mournful shadow of World War I still hung over mankind when Cassella first committed these characters to the page. That shadow suffuses two of the most riveting songs in the show, which detail the brief life and tragic death of Roberto, the Lambertis' son, in the Great War. In "Roberto's Eyes," Major Eric Fenton recalls, vividly and graphically, the dogfight that leads to the fiery demise of his flying partner. In the elegy "Losing Roberto," the Duchess Lamberti keeps troth with her absent son.

"How he loved winter!
Hiking he'd go
Leaving his footprints
Deep in the snow
They melt, but they're here with the rest
They melt, but not here in my breast…."

Jill Paice (Grazia) and Max von Essen (Corrado) with (left to right)
Don Stephenson (Fidele), Jay Jaski (Lorenzo), Rebecca Luker (Duchess Stephanie),
Michael Siberry (Duke Vittorio), and Patricia Noonan (Sophia)
"Life's a Joy"

And it is in witnessing this simple example of maternal sorrow that Death, astonishingly, is moved to pity. "I am sorry for your loss," he says to the Duchess.

In 1997, when Yeston and Stone began work on *Death Takes a Holiday,* they could hardly have imagined that the show would finally emerge into the light of day at a time as humid with mortality as that of its source material. America would be mired in two wars—in Iraq and Afghanistan. Intractable conflicts would be staining the earth with blood. The premiere of the musical would come just after the 30th anniversary of the first reported cases of AIDS, the start of an epidemic that would plunge the world in grief, and just before the 10th anniversary of the worst terrorist attack in history, which would claim the lives of 3,000 innocents. Even closer to home would be the death of Stone himself, in 2003, not to mention other friends and family members of the creative team. Death, it would seem, is in need of another vacation.

Until that twelfth of never, what the world does have is art. Art that says, as it does in this musical, that "in the middle of your life anything can happen." Art that says that love is the greatest journey that heaven can allow. And art that says that while the pain of loss is ineffable and unending, the beauty of music can give voice to that pain and even redeem it.

As Death himself sings:

"This remarkable grandeur
That fills you with wonderment
Love draw you in
With its light...
At least I got to live beneath the sun
To know of powers I've not understood
To learn how precious life may be
And understand the pain of ever leaving....
To learn it is a reservoir of light
And feel a love that roots me to this place
Whoever could have dreamed it would be life
I'd be most grateful for receiving...."

And then it is our turn to pity Death, to pity him for having been deprived from what we humans all too often take for granted. *Death Takes a Holiday* wittily and profoundly reminds us of this "precious" gift through Yeston's prodigious talent and the undiminished faith that infuses his every note and lyric.

CONTENTS

Kevin Earley (Death/Prince Sirki)
"I Thought That I Could Live"

How Will I Know?

Music and Lyrics by
Maury Yeston

B♭add9/F
In the mid - dle of that road, may - be an - y - thing did
F7sus4
hap - pen!
Cm7
For an in - stant, there was
F7sus4
Cm7
change, in a mo - ment bright and strange.
The fa - mil - iar
Am7♭5
D7sus4
D7
world I've al - ways rec - og - nized was
poco rit.
sim.

G9
gone... and, with it, all the con - fi - dence in
a tempo
sim.
F/G
G9
choic - es I have made that now I feel I can - not still re -
♩ = 105
F/G
G9sus4
G7
Cadd2
ly up - on... How will I know if the
rit.
Fadd9/A
G/B
Cadd9
Fadd9/A
G9sus4
G7
life I have cho - sen is the one meant to be for me? How will I
sim.

Cadd9 Fadd9/A G/B C Amsus4/2 Am
know if I'm des - tined for some - where far be - yond what my eyes can
Bb/C C9 Bb/C Fadd2 Dmsus4/2 Dm Dmsus4/2 Dm
see? No way to pre - dict the path that
B7sus4 B7 Eadd9 Bb7sus4 Bb7
leads me to the end. What if some - thing
Eb Cmsus4/2 Cm G7sus4 G7 Gm7b5 G7
deep - er is wait - ing out be - yond a - round the bend?
molto rit.

A♭7sus4
A♭7
A♭m7
A♭9sus4
A♭7
D♭add9
Life now seems so diff - 'rent! Some - how I know that the
ff
G♭add9/B♭
A♭/C
D♭add9
D♭
G♭add9/B♭
A♭9sus4
A♭7
world's more e - nor - mous than I dreamed it could ev - er be! Some - how I
sim.
D♭add9
G♭add9/B♭
A♭/C
D♭
B♭msus4/2
B♭m
know things I thought were im - pos - si - ble are pos - si - ble now for
C♭/D♭
D♭9
C♭/D♭
G♭add9
E♭msus4/2
E♭m
E♭msus4/2
E♭m
me! I flew through a wind that near - ly

C7sus4
C7
Fmaj9
B7sus4
B7
took my breath a - way!
Once I've tast - ed
E
C♯msus4/2
C♯m
G♯7sus4
G♯7
that, how could my life ev - er be the
rit.
G♯m7
G♯7
A♭9sus4 A♭7
D♭add9
G♭add9/B♭
A♭/C
same to - day? Oh! Now I know I must make ev - 'ry ef - fort to be
ff molto rit.
a tempo
D♭
B♭msus4/2
B♭m
F7sus4
F7
B♭m
B♭m/A♭
sure I will each day give the one life I have to
ff

E♭9/G
D♭/A♭
A♭7sus2
A♭7
live, a soul that will for - ev - er
D♭add9
F7/C
B♭m
B♭m/A♭
E♭9/G
grow! I won't rest un - til that's so, and
D♭/A♭
A♭
A♭7sus2
A♭7
A/C♯
fi - n'lly then, I'll tru - ly know!
rit.
ff
8va
Amaj7/C♯
D♭
8va
rit.

Centuries

Music and Lyrics by
Maury Yeston

F
Dm7
this.
toil.
Nev - er
Might I
G/D
F
once have I paused be - fore my i - cy
rest but a mo - ment to ex - plore earth's
Em
Dm7
G7
kiss.
soil?
E - ons I've per - formed my du - ties,
Fam - ines, earth - quakes, how they cost me!
poco rit.
a tempo
Cmaj7
Dm7
I've en - count - ered great - er beau - ties. What re - strains me
War and ill - ness, they ex - haust me. Would a res - pite

G7
Cmaj7
now, I won - der, feel - ing her heart race?
from my bur - den break e - ter - nal laws?
Em7
A7
Dmaj7
Stops my in - stinct to en - fold her, in the great war,
Ev - 'ry time they ven - ture near me, how they shud - der,
Em7
A7
not one sol - dier fell to me with quite the pow'r of
how they fear me. Could I come to life, just once, to
Very slowly
Em7
A7
C♯m
life with - in this face...
fi - n'lly learn the cause?
8va
molto rit.
mp

Why Do All Men?

Music and Lyrics by
Maury Yeston

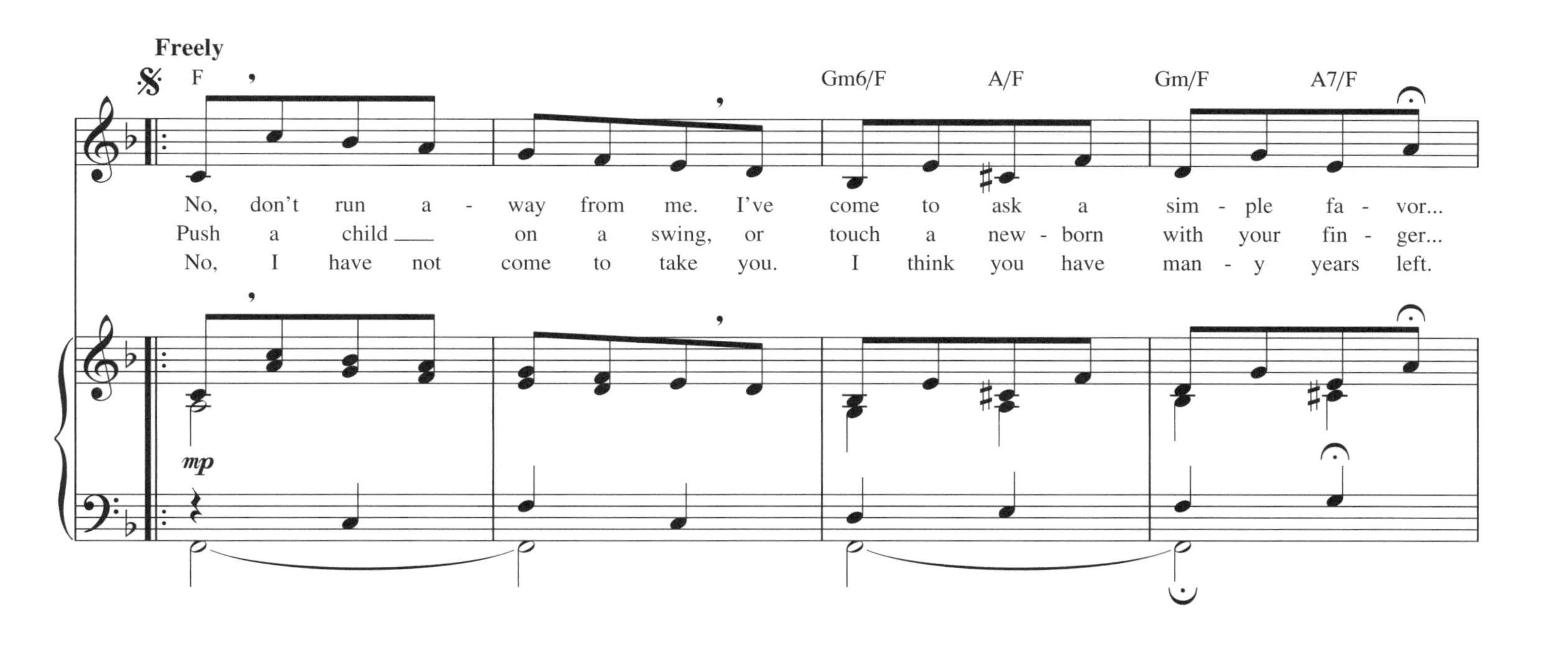
Freely
F
Gm6/F
A/F
Gm/F
A7/F
No, don't run a - way from me. I've come to ask a sim - ple fa - vor...
Push a child on a swing, or touch a new - born with your fin - ger...
No, I have not come to take you. I think you have man - y years left.
mp

F
Cm9/F
F9
Hear me out, I beg you to com - ply. Though I'm ex -
How I have been tan - ta - lized to try! What could that
Treat me as a house guest in Ju - ly. If I could

B♭maj9
B♭m6/D♭
act - ly who you think I'd be, I'm here from cu - ri - os - i - ty. Be -
be? I've not a clue, to be in - side the world of you, I can't i -
learn what words like "hope" and "love" and "kind - ness" tru - ly are made of... If

F/C
G9
lieve me, I don't want to hurt a fly...
mag - ine what it's like to breathe a sigh...
I could learn what it may be to cry...

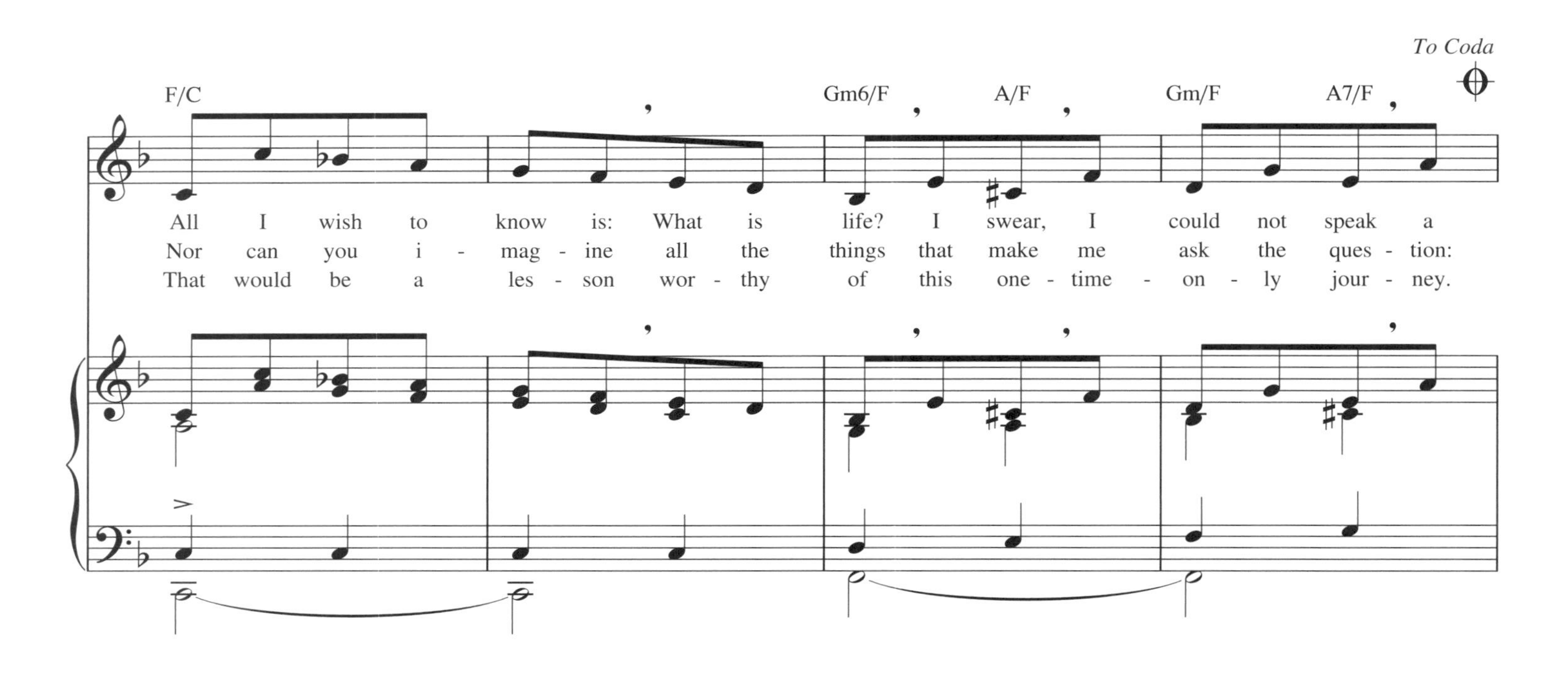
To Coda
F/C
Gm6/F
A/F
Gm/F
A7/F
All I wish to know is: What is life? I swear, I could not speak a
Nor can you i - mag - ine all the things that make me ask the ques - tion:
That would be a les - son wor - thy of this one - time - on - ly jour - ney.

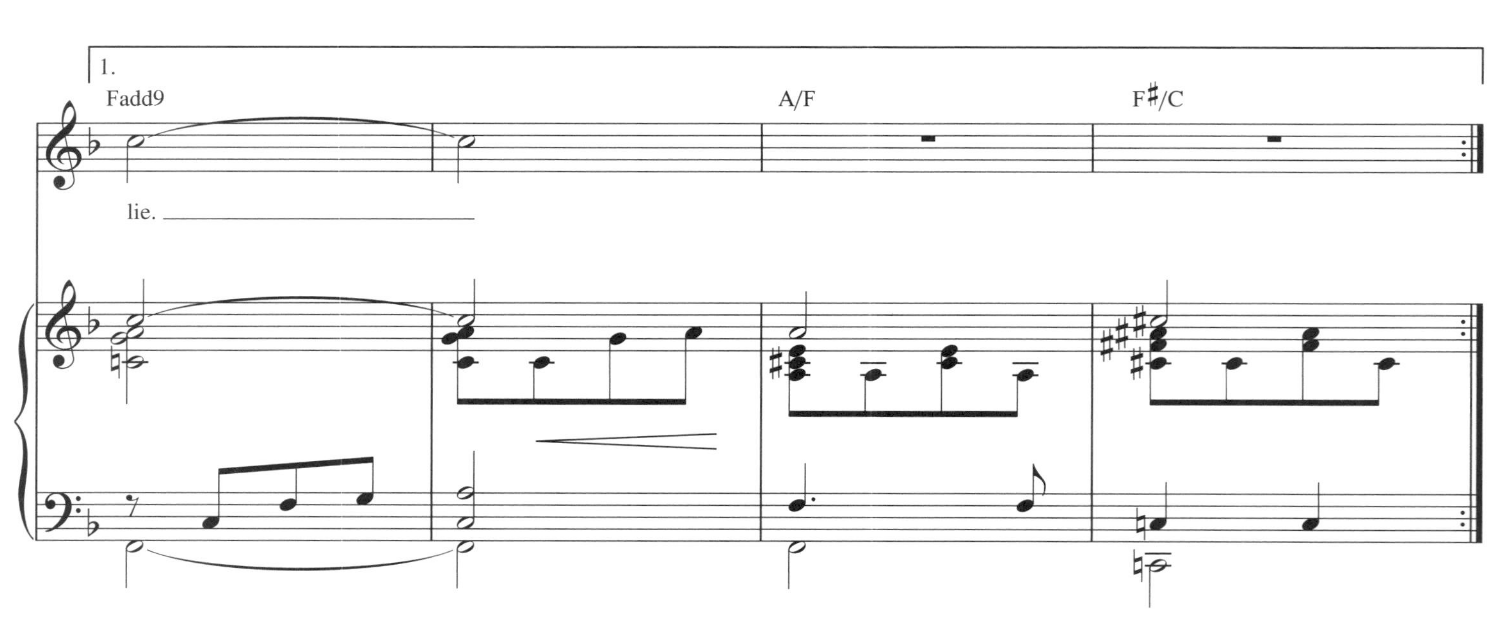
1.
Fadd9
A/F
F♯/C
lie.

2.
Poco agitato
Fadd9
A7sus4
A7
why?
a tempo
rit.
♩ = 96
Dm
Gm6/D
Why do all men fear me?
Cling to life so dear - ly?
mp a tempo
mf
mp
Ped.
sim.
Dm
B♭7/D
What is it they fear they'd lose?
mf
mp
E♭
A7
Dmsus4/2
Why have I be - come the dread - ed spec - ter all men see?

Bm7♭5 Dm/E E7 Am Dm6/A
I must know their rea - sons, live their change of sea - sons,
Am F7/A B♭
see my pres - ence from their view. That is why I now in -
Gm A♭ Gm/D D7sus4 D7 Gm
tend to spend a lit - tle hol - i - day with you!
rit.
C9sus4 Fmaj7/C
I'll be here two days, then I will be gone.
mf a tempo
f
mf
mf

C9sus4
Gm7
Mid - night, Sun - day night,
that's my on - ly goal.
D.S. al Coda
B♭/C Am/C B♭/C Am/C Gm/C F/C C7
I'll not harm a soul...
rall.
poco rit.
Coda
Slowly ♩ = 40
Gm6/F A/F Gm/F A7/F Gm6/F A/F Gm/F A7/F Fadd9
In re - turn, I can as - sure you: while I'm here, no one on earth will die!
8va
mp
rit.
a tempo
F♯/C
F

Death Is in the House

Music and Lyrics by
Maury Yeston

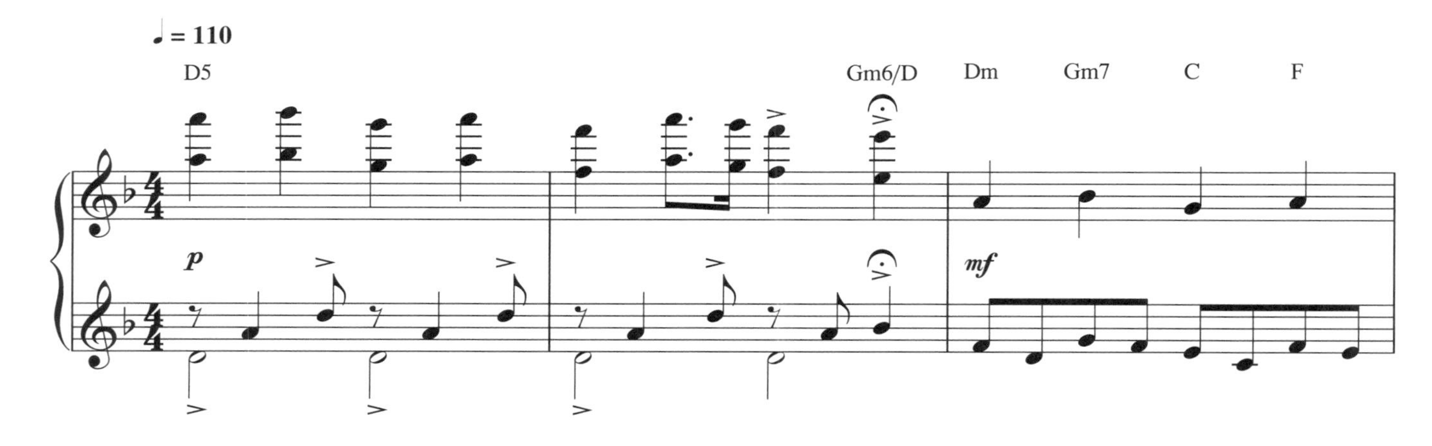

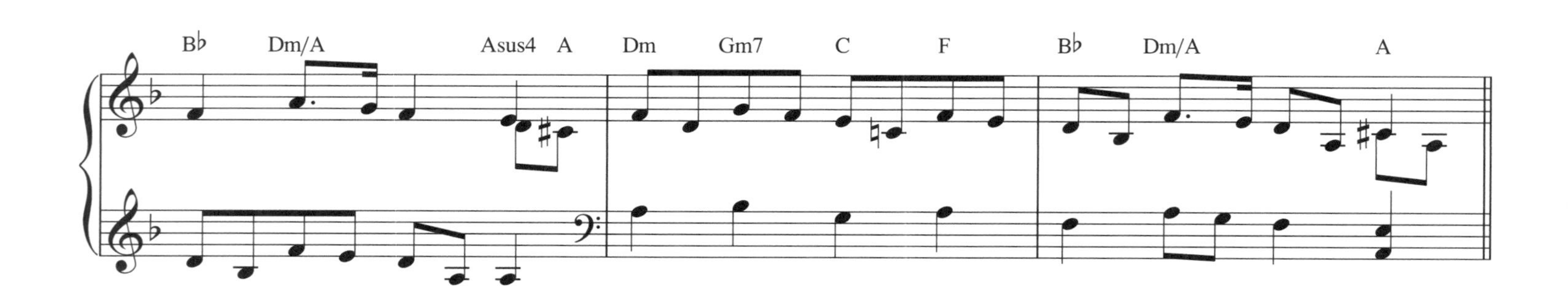

*Can be performed as a solo.

B♭
Dm/G
Dm/A
A
Dm
Gm/D
Gm6/D
Dm
He is in the house.
bring-ing on this fear I've got. He is in the house, wheth - er he's a
B♭
Dm/G
Dm/A
A
F/A
C
Dm
C
Am/C
What does it mat - ter?
man or a night - mare, What does it mat - ter?
f
8vb
F/A
C
Dm
C
Can we be - lieve him?
Can we be - lieve him?

Am
Dm/A
Dm6/A
Am
Fadd9
Am7/D
Am/E
E7
Death is in the house. Ahh!
Death is in the house; none of us is safe or se - cure now.
mf
I will not sleep sound. Ahh!
I will not sleep sound pon - der - ing what we may en - dure now.
Dm
Gm7
C
F
B♭
Dm/G
Dm/A
A
Death! House! Or shad - ow.
Death, Death is in the house, Wheth - er he's a sym - bol or shad - ow

Dm Gm/D Gm6/D Dm Bb Dm/G F/A C7
Where can we go?
wear-ing his dark robe, when he points to us, where can we go?
F/A C Dm C Dm
Who would be-lieve what we saw with our eyes? We could nev-er
What does it mat - ter?
ff
F/A C Dm C
tell what he looks like!
What he may look like!

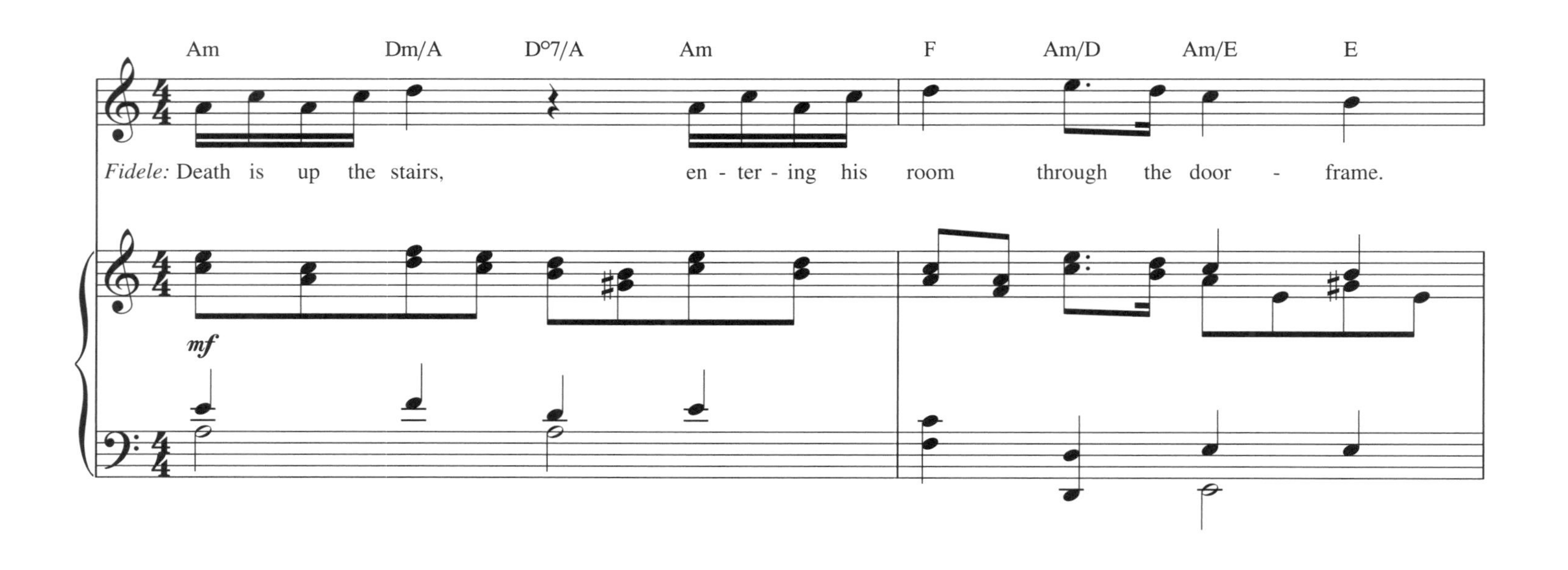
Am
Dm/A
D°7/A
Am
F
Am/D
Am/E
E
Fidele: Death is up the stairs, en - ter - ing his room through the door - frame.
mf

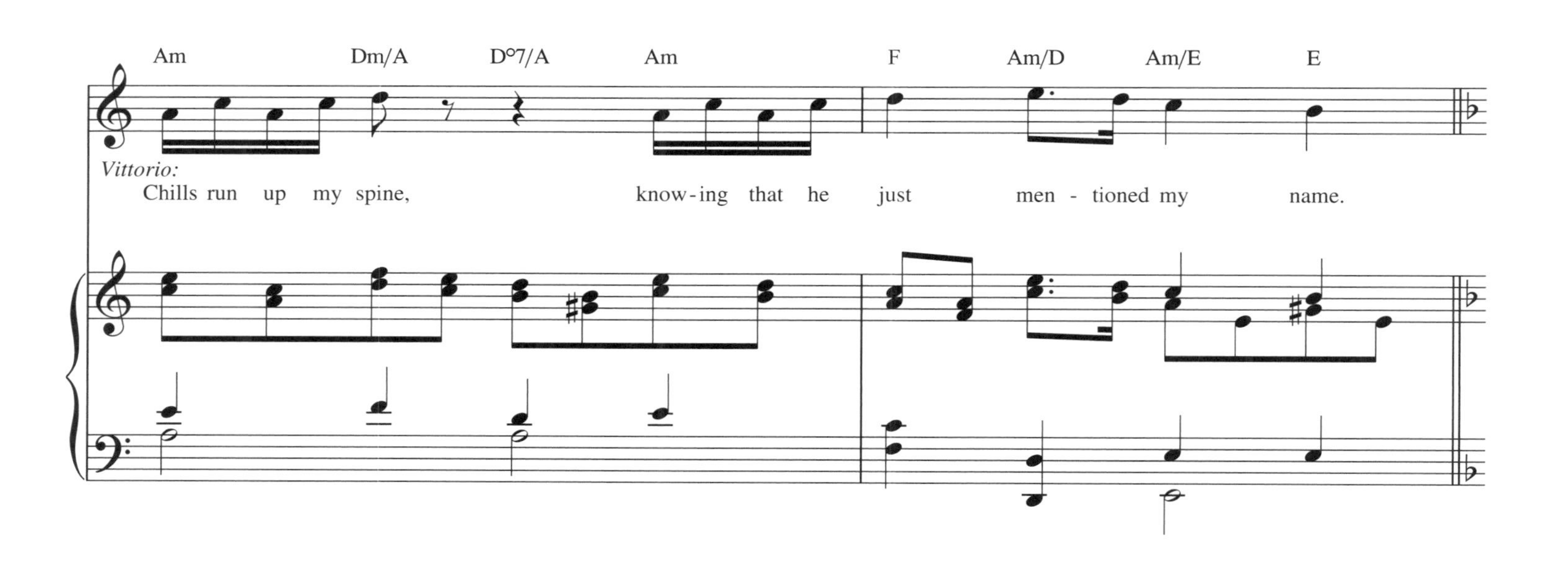
Am
Dm/A
D°7/A
Am
F
Am/D
Am/E
E
Vittorio:
Chills run up my spine, know-ing that he just men - tioned my name.

Dm7
Gm7
C
F
B♭
Dm/G
Dm/A
A
Fidele: Death! House!
Vittorio:
Death! Death is in the house, wheth - er he's a man or a night - mare,
sub. p

Dm Gm/D C/D Dm7 G F G F G A
Vittorio:
Death is in the house and he picked to - night to come call - ing.
F/A C Dm C Dm
Fidele: Wak - ing or dream - ing,
Vittorio: Wak - ing or dream - ing,
F/A C Dm C
I feel his pres - ence.
I feel his pres - ence.

Am Dm/A Dm6/A Am F Am/D Am/E E7 Dm7 Gm7 C F
Vittorio: No way we can run! What is to be done? And we must re -
mp
f
molto rit.
Bb Dm/G Dm/F Asus4 A
Slowly
A tempo
D5
veal this to no one. Fidele: Death is in this house.
mp
Slowly
A tempo
Gm6/D
D5
Vittorio: Death is in my house!
ff
Gm6/D C/D D5
poco rit.
sfz
sfz

Alive!

Music and Lyrics by
Maury Yeston

Em/A
Look! Here's a rose! Do you sup - pose

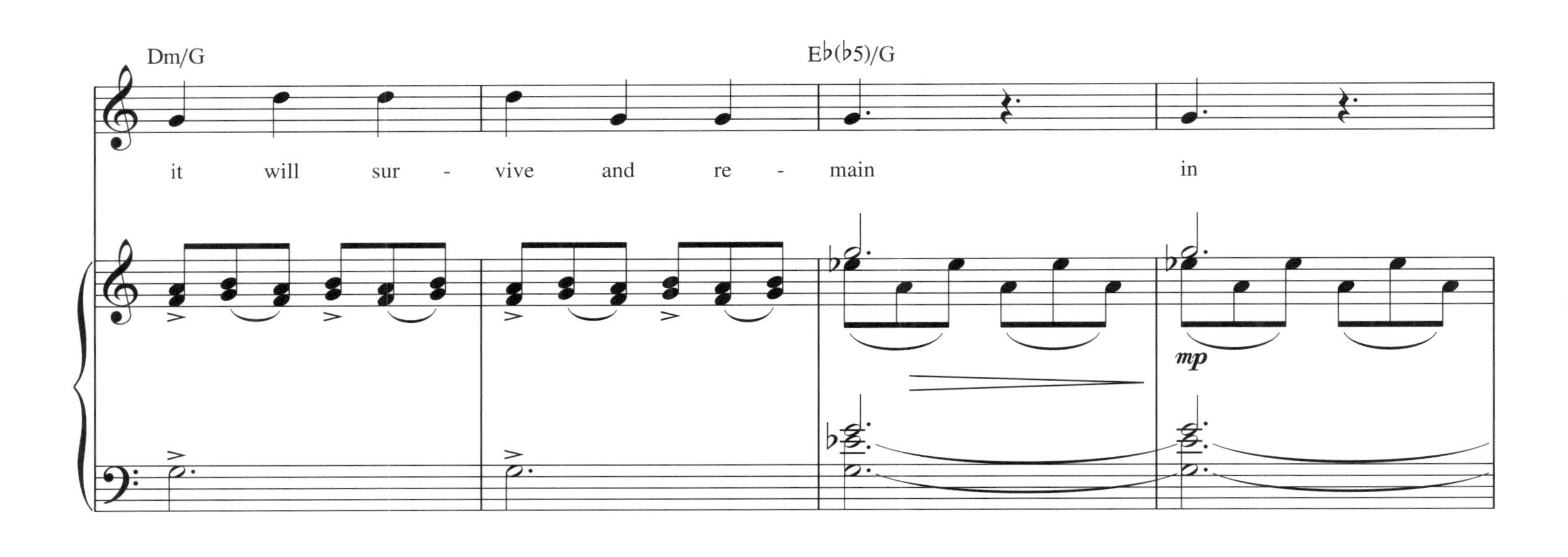
Dm/G
Eb(b5)/G
it will sur - vive and re - main in
mp

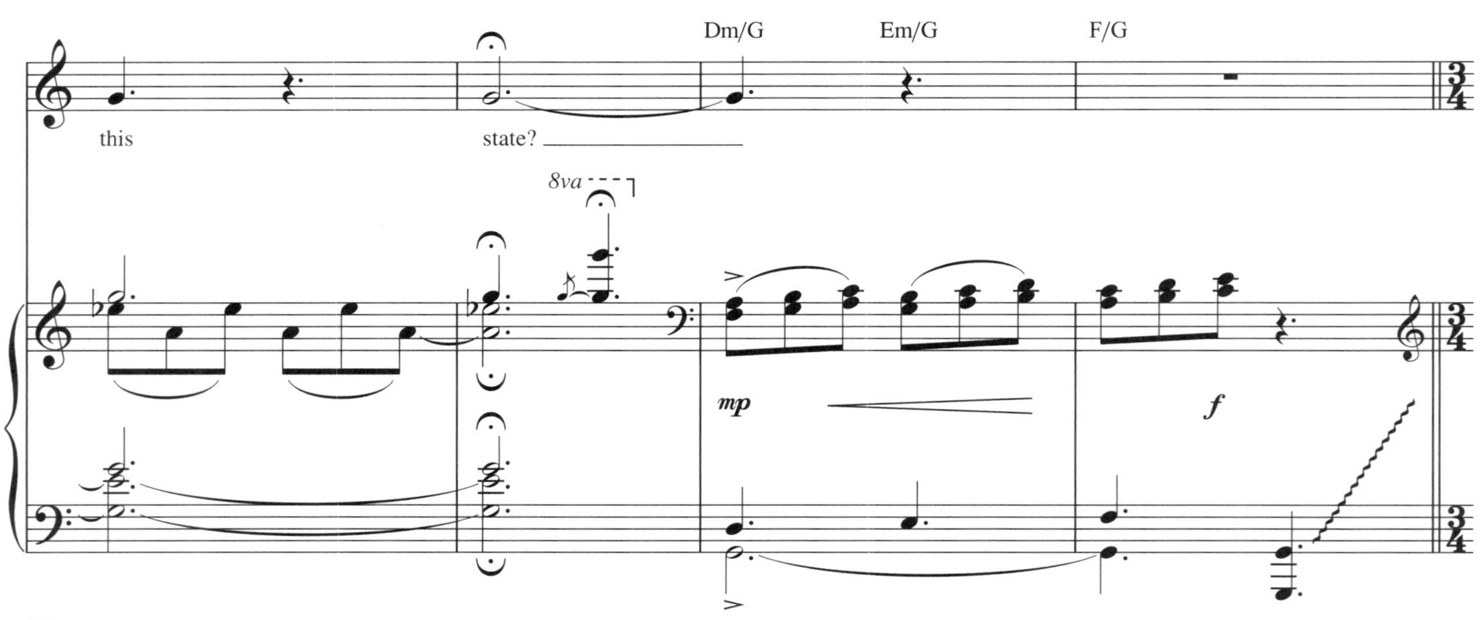
Dm/G
Em/G
F/G
this state?
8va
mp
f

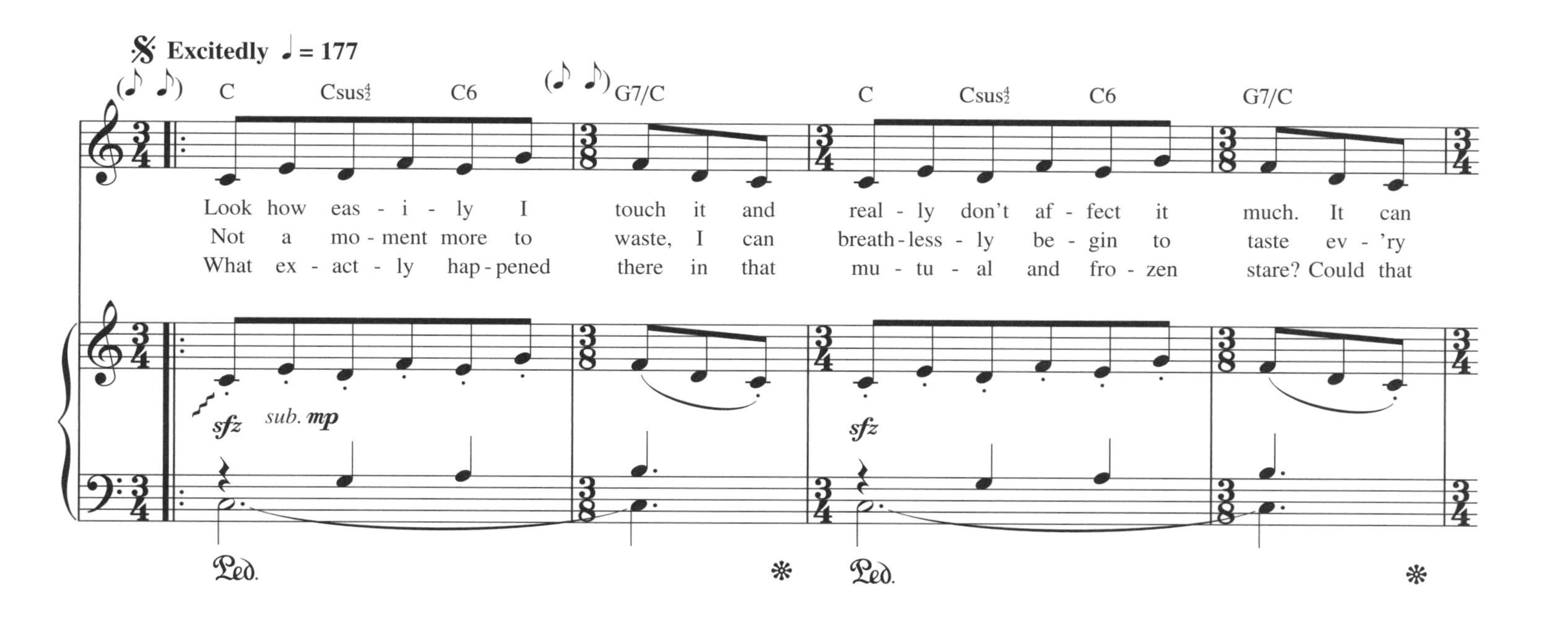
Excitedly ♩ = 177
C Csus4/2 C6 G7/C C Csus4/2 C6 G7/C
Look how eas - i - ly I touch it and real - ly don't af - fect it much. It can
Not a mo - ment more to waste, I can breath - less - ly be - gin to taste ev - 'ry
What ex - act - ly hap - pened there in that mu - tu - al and fro - zen stare? Could that
sfz sub. mp
sfz

C Csus4/2 C6 G7/C C5
clear - ly be ob - served that it's still a - live!
sight and sound and smell that may soon ar - rive…
in - stant of at - trac - tion grow and sur - vive?
8va
sfz
sfz
f

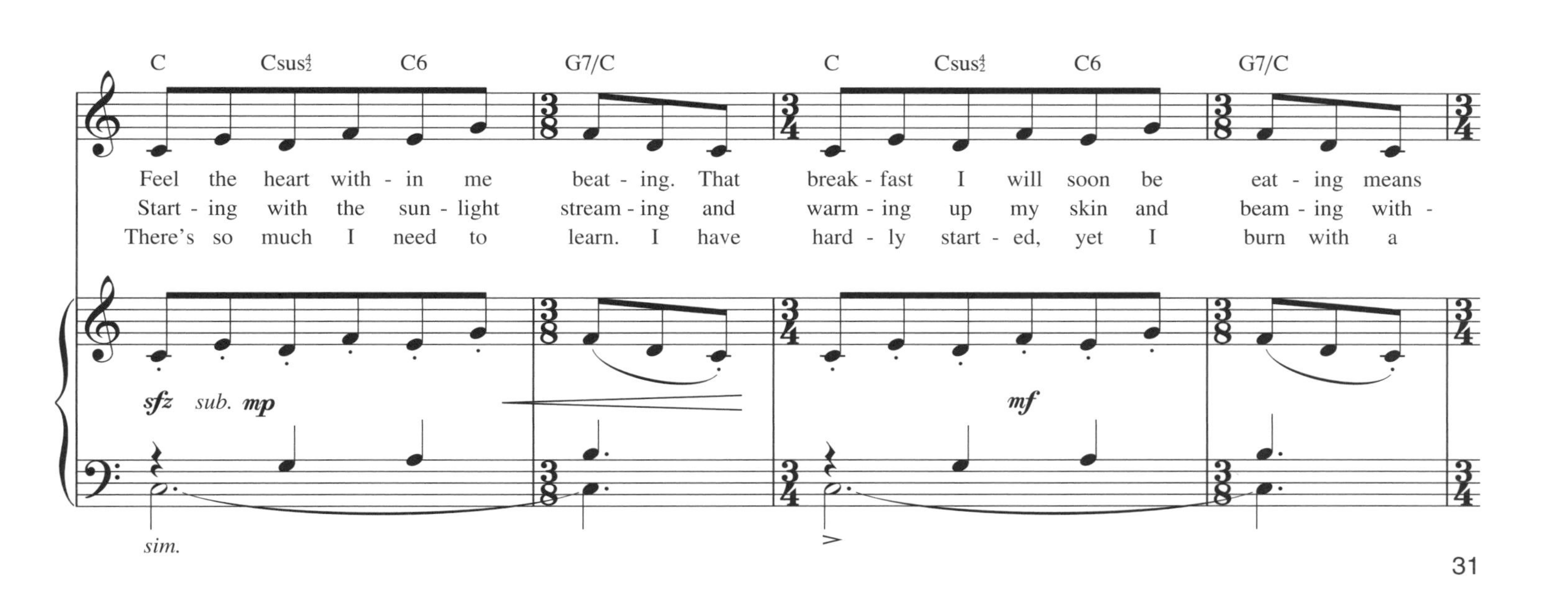
C Csus4/2 C6 G7/C C Csus4/2 C6 G7/C
Feel the heart with - in me beat - ing. That break - fast I will soon be eat - ing means
Start - ing with the sun - light stream - ing and warm - ing up my skin and beam - ing with -
There's so much I need to learn. I have hard - ly start - ed, yet I burn with a
sfz sub. mp
mf
sim.

C Csus4/2 C6 G7/C Gm/C C
I am, as I keep re - peat-ing, a - live!
in me this new glow of com-ing a - live!
pas-sion-ate and un-mis - tak-a-ble drive!
f
cresc.

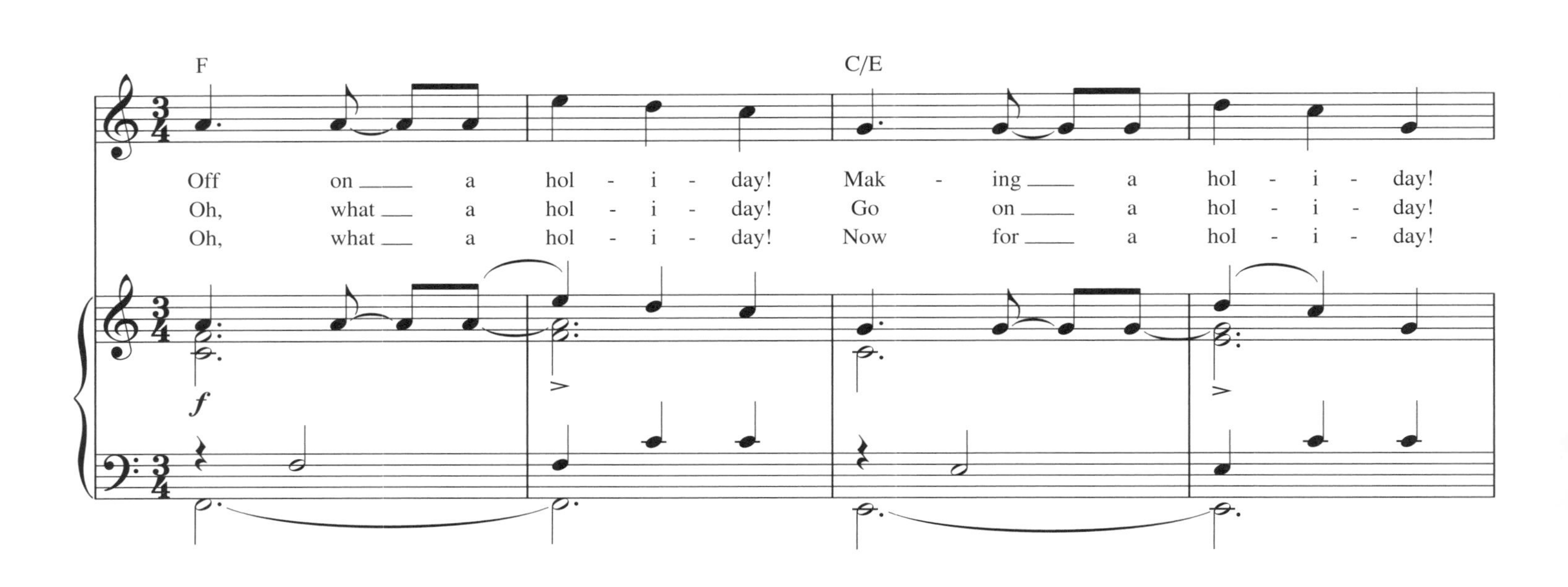
F C/E
Off on a hol - i - day! Mak - ing a hol - i - day!
Oh, what a hol - i - day! Go on a hol - i - day!
Oh, what a hol - i - day! Now for a hol - i - day!
f

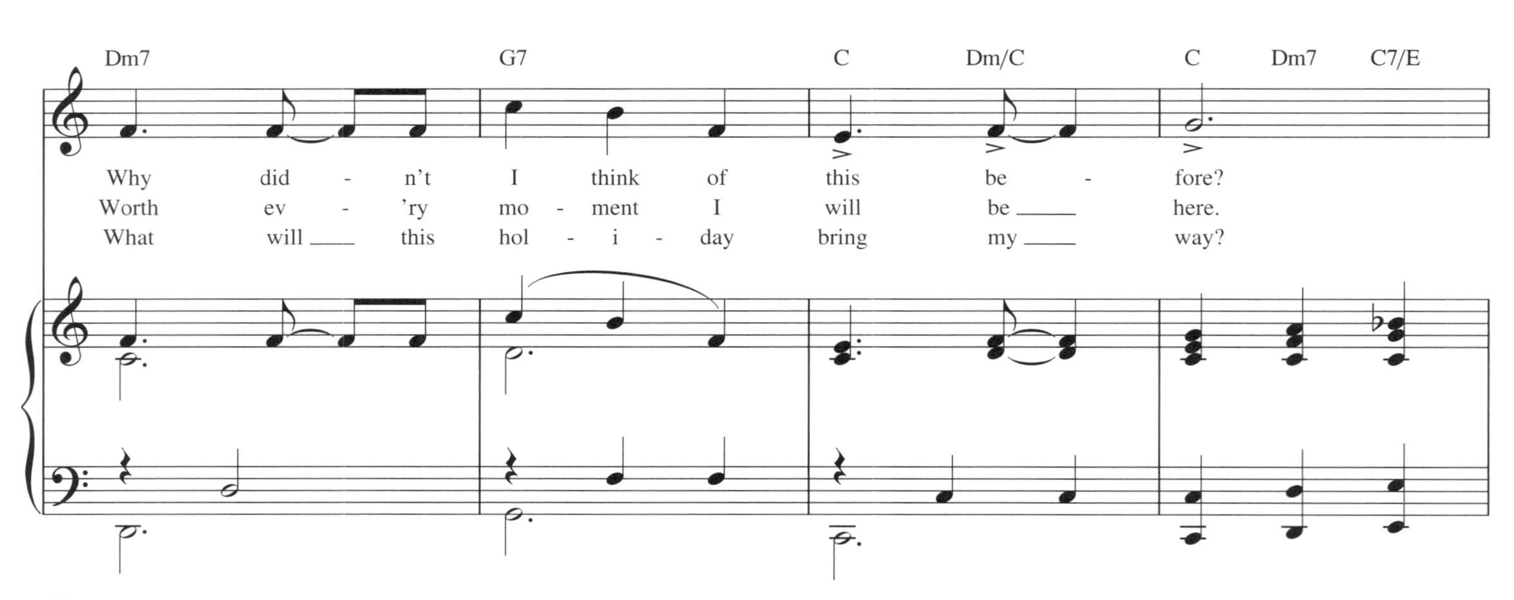
Dm7 G7 C Dm/C C Dm7 C7/E
Why did - n't I think of this be - fore?
Worth ev - 'ry mo - ment I will be here.
What will this hol - i - day bring my way?

To Coda
F
C/E
How could I not have known what would be wait - ing in
Fill ev - 'ry min - ute and thrill as the won - ders ap -
Could all the plans I've de - signed now de - vel - op and
Bb
Bbsus2
G7sus4
1.
2.
D/G
store?…
pear!
The
Em9
se - cret mys - ter - y of life
I've
Fmaj9#11
Fmaj7
nev - er quite de - fined
could

Em9
soon un - fold to be re - vealed
and
sub. mp
mf
Fmaj9♯11
Fadd9
o - pen to my mind!
E♭/G
Dm/G
Em/G
F/G
rit. poco a poco
mp
mf
f
C
Csus4
C6
G7/C
Look! A fer - ry boat's gone un - der, the pass - en - gers are thrown as -
mf
sfz

G7/C
C
Csus4/2
C6
G7/C
sun - der, and ev - 'ry sin - gle one of them still a -
C5
C
Csus4/2
C6
G7/C
live!...
8va
Here, a speed - ing train's de - rail - ing and
f
mf
C
Csus4/2
C6
G7/C
C
Csus4/2
C6
(Shouted)
there, a sick - ly fel - low's ail - ing and ev - 'ry bless - ed one of
f
G7/C
Gm/C
C
them is a - live!
cresc.

F
C/E
Time for a hol - i - day! I'm on a hol - i - day,
f
Dm7
G7
C
Dm/C
C
Dm7
C7/E
new and phe - nom - e - nal way to be!
F
C/E
No way to know what the next mo - ment's hold - ing for
f
B♭
B♭sus2
G7sus4
D/G
me!
ff

Em9
Fmaj9♯11
Fmaj7
Dm/G
Em/G
mp
F/G
D.S. al Coda
f
Coda
B♭
B♭sus2
G7sus4
thrive?
ff
p
A♭/G♭
sfz

C/G
Dm/G
Cu - ri - os - i - ty will win the day, fol - low - ing the role I
sfz
mp
cresc.
C/G
F/G
G
Am/G
said I'd play, be - ing on hol - i - day, hol - i - day, hol - i - day
f
cresc.
G
C
Csus4/2
C6
G7/C
C
Csus4/2
C6
while I'm a - live!
ff
G7/C
C
Csus4/2
C6
G
C5
fff
sffz

Life's a Joy

Music and Lyrics by
Maury Yeston

Cm F7 B♭maj7 B♭6 G13 C6
older, I'm bolder to say: Life prevails
where,
in details,
Grazia: ev'ry where,
C7
tiny moments that make up your
Both: fragrant flowers awaken and
Fmaj7 F6 D/F♯ D°/F C/E
day. In the grand scheme of things, what's a dragonfly's
play. Grazia: Through the groves of the pines, how the blue water
sim.
C°/E♭ Dm7 G7 Cmaj7 C7
wings but a minor diaphanous toy? Till it
shines, casting light beams no shade can destroy, Sirki: till each

D/F♯
D°/F
C/E
C°/E♭
Dm7
brush - es your face with mi - rac - u - lous grace and you real - ize your
wave - let now gleams bright as dia - monds, it seems, Both: and you real - ize your
To Coda
G7
C
Gm7
B♭/C
C7
life is a joy!
All: An - cient Ro - man
life is a
3
f
Fadd9
Gm7
B♭/C
C7
Fadd9
foun - tains,
palm trees near the lake,
Am7
C/D
D7
Gadd9
dis - tant snow - capped moun - tains,
41

Am7 C/D D9 Dm/G Em/G F/G G7 B♭7
what a view they make!
Half the group: Life's a
sfz
sfz
ff
E♭6
joy! Pass - ing by... Life is ap - ples and
The other half: A - long the La - go, As we go stroll - ing,
F♯o7 Fm7 B♭7 Fm
lem - ons and lime trees. To - tal joy to the
A - long the La - go,
3

A♭/B♭
B♭9
Fm
B♭7
E♭maj7
eye, bril - liant col - ors in sweet dis - ar - ray.
the day un - fold - ing,
(3)
E♭6
G13
C6
Dario: Ev - 'ry - where,
All: ev - 'ry - where, all your
sub. mp
f
C7
Fmaj7
F6
D/F♯
trou - bles slip slow - ly a - way, and you stare till you
D°/F
C/E
C°/E♭
Dm7
G7
sigh at the world pass - ing by, and you real - ize your life is a
(3)

Somewhat freely
C
E♭/F
F13
B♭6
joy!
Grazia: Life's a joy!
poco rit.
B♭maj7
B♭6
C♯°7
Sirki: Life's a joy!
Grazia: Gold - en sun - light creeps up on the
Cm7
F7
Cm
E♭/F
La - go.
Life's a joy!
Sirki: What a joy,
D.S. al Coda
F9
Cm
F9
B♭maj7
B♭6
G13
be - ing part of the start of the day.
Ev - 'ry -

Coda
C
B♭7
joy!
Half the group: Life's a
rit.
E♭6
joy!
Pass - ing by...
Life is ap - ples and
The other half: A - long the La - go,
as we go stroll - ing.

F♯°7
Fm7
B♭7
Fm
lem - ons and lime trees.
To - tal joy to the
A - long the La - go,
3

A♭/B♭
B♭9
Fm
B♭7
E♭maj7
eye,
All: bril - liant
col - ors
in
sweet
dis
-
ar
-
ray.
the day un - fold - ing,

A bit slower
E♭6
G13
C6
C7
Dario: Ev - 'ry
-
where,
Sirki: ev - 'ry - where
faint a - ro - mas
re -
sub. mp
rit.

Slowly, freely
Fmaj7
F6
D/F♯
D°/F
C/E
veal
their
bou
-
quet.
Dario: As you're
gaz - ing
on
high
at
a
Tie - po
-
lo

C°/E♭
Dm7
G7
Cmaj7
C7
D/F♯
sky, All: think - ing there are no words to em - ploy Dario: that will cap-ture a -
3
p
D°/F
C/E
C°/E♭
Dm7
loud ev - 'ry wisp of each cloud, All: or the feel - ing your
rit.
mp
sub. f a tempo
F/G
G7sus4
C
life is a joy!
sfz
fff
sfz
accel.

Who Is This Man?

Music and Lyrics by
Maury Yeston

B♭7sus4 A♭maj7/B♭ B♭7
ly.
E♭ B♭7 B♭7/E♭ E♭
Try - ing not to think of him, I fail,
Gmadd9 A♭maj9 E♭add9/B♭ Cm Gm7♭5 Gm7♭5/C C7
and, be - side him, all else seems to pale.
Slower
Fm A♭add9
Bolt out of the blue.
poco rit.
Even slower
Cm Am7♭5
In - con - ven - ient, too!
A tempo
E♭add9/B♭ A♭/B♭ Gm/B♭
And ab - so - lute - ly riv - et - ing my sens - es.
E♭add9/B♭ A♭/B♭ B♭7sus4 B♭7
Break - ing down the last of my de - fens - es.
molto rit.
E♭
I can - not hide what I feel from
a tempo

D♭/E♭ E♭add9 A♭add9 A♭add9/G Fm7 B♭7
Sir - ki. Play that role...
E♭ D♭/E♭ E♭add9 A♭add9 A♭/B♭ B♭7
Ev-'ry tossed-off word he ut-ters takes its toll...
Gm7♭5 Gm7♭5/C C7 Fm C7/G A♭maj7 Fm/A♭
Some-how I can't keep my prom - ise to Cor - ra - do,
Am7♭5 D7sus4 D7 Gmaj9 B♭7sus4 A♭/B♭ B♭9
wait-ing in the wings to hold an ea - ger bride. For
rit.

E♭
A♭/C
D♭/F
E♭/G
A♭add9
A♭add9/G
F9
there's an - oth - er per - son who keeps loom - ing in - to view.
a tempo
f
sfz
E♭/B♭
B♭7sus4
B♭7
E♭/B♭
What if I'm a fi - re - fly he's caught?
Glow - ing on the edg - es of his
sfz
f
rit.
Slower
A tempo
E/B♭
B♭7sus2
B♭7
Fm7
A♭/B♭
B♭13
E♭
thought?
Dear prince, what would my life be if I loved you?
molto rit.
mp
A♭
B♭7
B♭7/E♭
E♭
Nev - er have I known so lit - tle doubt.
rit.
a tempo

Gmadd9 A♭maj9 E♭add9/B♭ Cm Gm7♭5 Gm7♭5/C C7 Fm A♭add9
Some - how he is who my life's a - bout. What am I to do
poco rit.
Slower
Cm Am7♭5 E♭add9/B♭ A♭/B♭ Gm/B♭ Dm7♭5/A♭
if my heart speaks true? And, dear prince, what would my life be if I loved... Oh,
poco accel.
E♭add9/G A♭ D/A E♭add9/B♭ F7/C
Freely
E♭/B♭
is it pos - si - ble you could be my love? Oh, tell me what would my life be if
A♭maj7/B♭ B♭9 E♭ A♭ B♭7 E♭
I loved you?
p
mf
f
molto rit.

Shimmy Like They Do in Paree

Music and Lyrics by
Maury Yeston

A13
dance your blues a - way.
B13
We'll shake and shim - my, push-ing the
E9
bounds of taste.
A13
Now take your arm and put it a -
D9♭5
round my
D9♯5
waist, and
G
glide
F♯+
me
F6
on
E7
that
E♭maj7
pol -
E7
ished
F6
floor.
F♯+
G

A13
We can't want for more.
Cadd9
E♭maj7♯5
G/D
E7
As we ex - plore how naugh - ty we can be, we'll
sfz
sfz
A7
D7
G
F♯+
F6
shim - my like they do in Pa - ree.
Instrumental...
p
E7
E♭maj7
D
E♭maj7
E7
F6
F♯+
3

G6/9
Shim - my on the left, shim - my on the right, let me see you shim - my up to me.
A13
Cud - dle on the left, cud - dle on the right, lem - me see how cud - dly you can be.
B13
E9♭5
E9
Snug - gle up, snug - gle up, come on, get clos - er!
sfz
A13
D9♭5
D9♯5
Snug - gle up, snug - gle up, I won't say no sir! Now
sfz

G6/9
shim-my once a-gain, shim-my once a-gain, lem-me see you shim-my at the knee.
A13
Si-dle up a-gain, si-dle up a-gain while you are si-dling up to me.
Cadd9
E♭maj7♯5
G/D
E7
Give it a try, ex-plore how in-ti-mate we can be! We'll
sfz
sfz
A7
D7
G
F♯+
F6
E7
A9
shim-my like they do in Pa-... We'll shim-my like they do in Pa-... We'll shim-my like they do
cresc.

C6/D
in
Pa-...
sfz
cresc.
ff
C/D
Db/D
D
Eb/D
C/D
Db/D
f
cresc.
D
Eb/D
E/D
F/D
F#/D
G/D
Ab/D
G6/9
Alice: A - one and two and three and four!
Shim - my on the left, shim - my
Sirki: Liv - en
ff
on the right, let me see you shim - my up to me.
up your feet to - day;
A13
Cud - dle on the left, cud - dle
dance your

B13
on the right, lem - me see how cud - dly you can be.
Snug - gle up,
blues a - way.
We'll shake and
E9♭5
E9
A13
snug - gle up, come on, get clos - er!
Snug - gle up,
shim - my, push - ing the bounds of taste.
Now take your
sfz
D9♭5
D9♯5
snug - gle up, I won't say no sir! Now shim - my once a - gain, shim - my
arm and put it a - round my waist, and glide me
sfz

A13
once a-gain, lem-me see you shim-my at the knee.
Si-dle up a-gain, si-dle
on that pol-ished floor.
We can't
up a-gain while you are si-dling up to me.
Cadd9
Give it a try, ex-
want for more.
Give it a try, ex-
E♭maj7♯5
G/D
E7
A7
plore how in-ti-mate we can be!
We'll shim-my like they do
plore how in-ti-mate we can be!
We'll shim-my like they do
sfz
sfz

D7
G
F#+
F6
E7
A9
in Pa-... We'll shim - my like they do in Pa-... We'll shim - my like they do
in Pa-... We'll shim - my like they do in Pa-... We'll shim - my like they do
cresc.
C6/D
G
G#
A
B♭
B
C
in Pa - ree!
in Pa - ree!
ff
sfz
3
cresc.
C#
D
E♭
E
F
F#
G
G#
A
B♭
B
C
E♭
E
F
F#
G

Roberto's Eyes

Music and Lyrics by
Maury Yeston

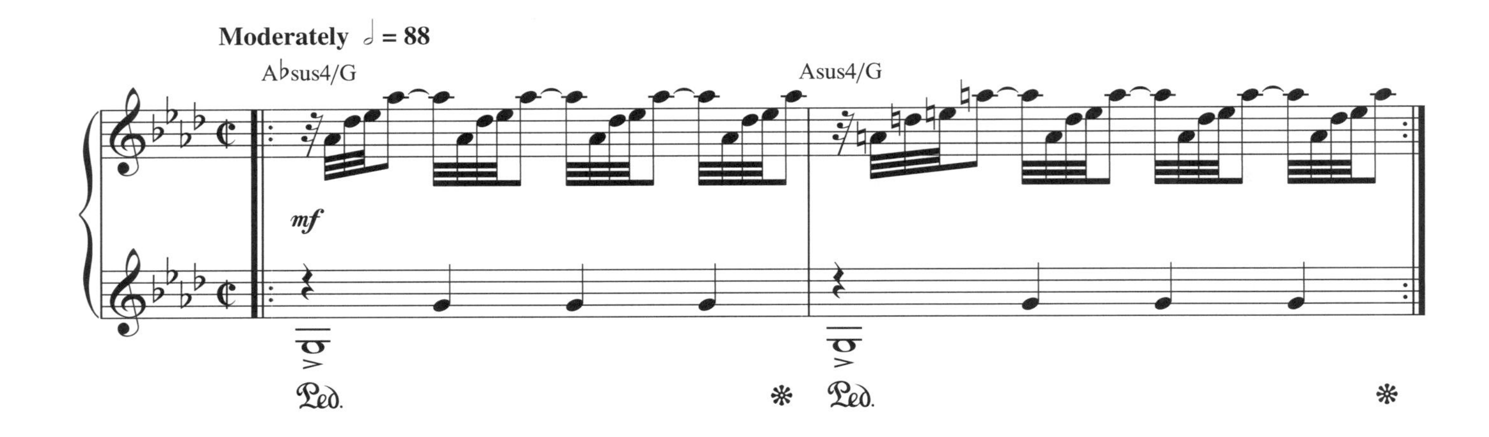

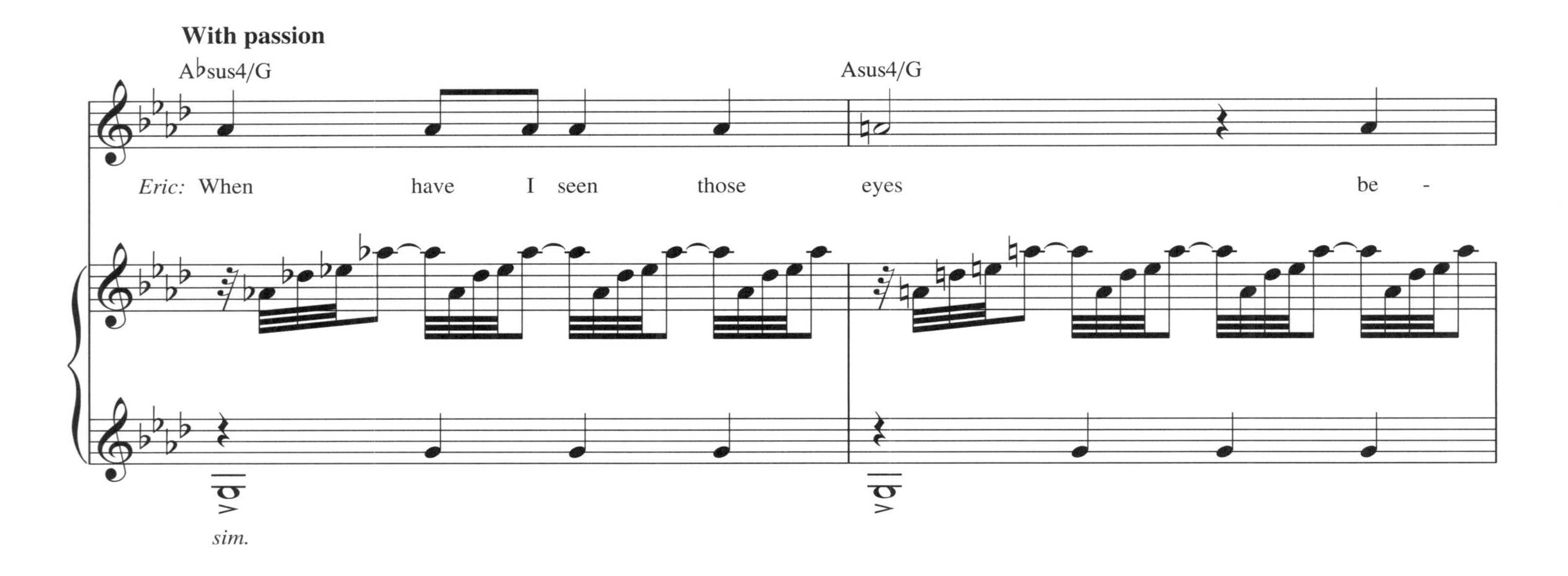

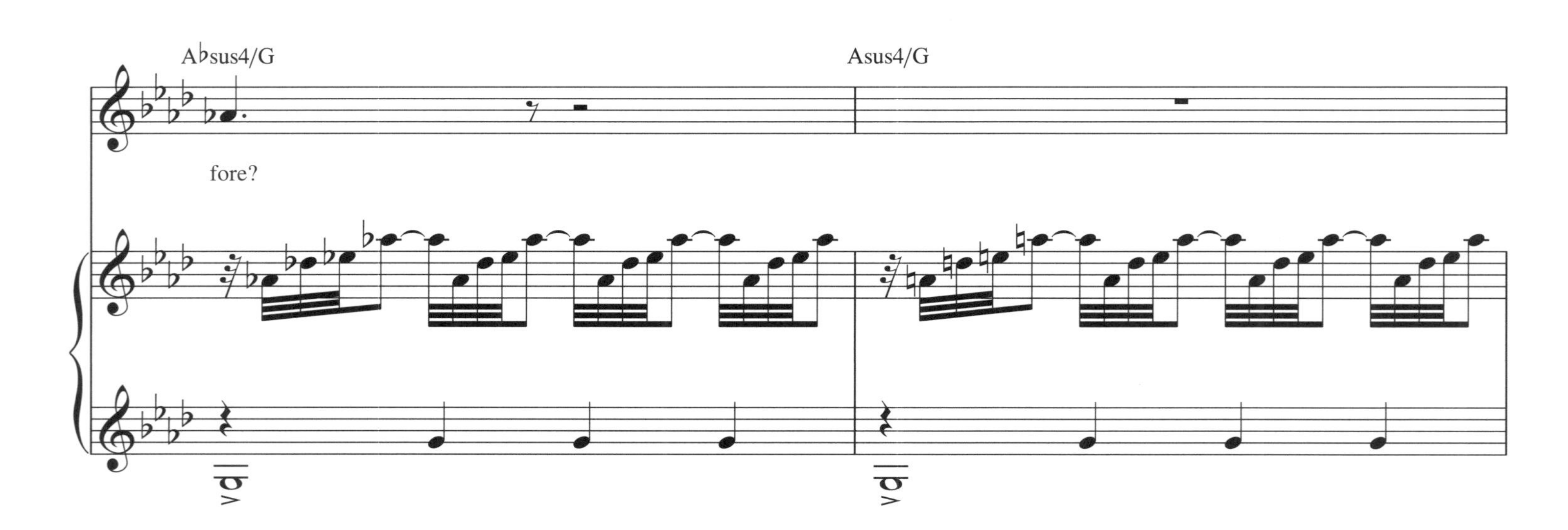

Absus4/G
Asus4/G
Some - where I've seen those eyes be -
fore!
G11
Ag - es a - go, far up a - bove, feel - ing the wind rush...
mp
sim.
Some - thing a - bout the look of him brings me back to then...

B9sus4
Feel the con - trols, hand on the stick, fly - ing a bi - plane...
Bris - tol F - 2
fight - er...
Wing - man to Ro - ber - to...
Eadd9/G♯
E/G♯
Bsus4/A
B7
High a - bove the clouds...
Cut - ting through the
Eadd9/G♯
E/G♯
Emadd9/G
Em/G
air...

B/F♯
F7♭5
in
the
E
E7♭9
war...
rit.
f
Slower
Am7
Pi - lot - ing his Bris - tol sev - en thou - sand feet a - loft,
He can out - ma - neu - ver him; he's got him on the run.
sailing like a glider
mf
Ped.
Ped. sim.
Dm7
G13
Cmaj7
chas - ing down a Ger - man plane whose tail he's set a - blaze,
Then the Ger - man rolls and points his nose in - to the sun.

Bm7♭5 B♭7 Am7 Dm Bm7♭5 Em7
Jer - ry dodg - es left and right; Ro - ber - to's like a cat. His gun sight
Blind - ed for a sec - ond now, Ro - ber - to loops a - bove, un - til there's
Ped. ❊ Ped. ❊
Am G Fmaj7 Fadd9
nev - er los - es track of where he flies... When
noth - ing all a - round but emp - ty skies... When
1.
Dm Em7 Am9sus4 Am7
was it when I looked in - to those eyes? When
was it when I last be - held those
Dm Em7 Am
was it when I last be - held those eyes?

2.
Am9sus4
Am7
E♭11
eyes?
Then all at once, there dead a head, high in the
ff
heav - ens...
Both of them race there,
face to face, no way to turn back...
One of them will

A♭add9/C
A♭/C
E♭sus4/D♭
E♭
live...
One of them will
ff
A♭add9/C
A♭/C
A♭madd9/C♭
A♭m/C♭
die...
E♭/B♭
F7♭5
Fmaj7♭5
It
was
8vb
E
E7♭9
war...
rit.
f

With intensity
Am
Left and right, his wings are shred-ding, sit - u - a - tion
mf a tempo
sfz
dire!
Dm7
Now Ro - ber - to's shoot-ing back; there's
G13
Cmaj7
Bm7♭5
hard - ly time to fire...
Then a Ger - man
B♭7
Am7
Dm
Bm7♭5
Em7
bul-let hits di - rect - ly in his en - gine and Ro -

Am
G
Fmaj7
ber - to's in a tail - spin trail - ing smoke.
f
Fadd9
Amsus4/2
Am
I fol - low as he falls...
mf
Fadd9
He turns to me and waves...
mp
F
Em7add4
Em7
A smile be - trays his ter - ror...

C/E
Fadd9
I stare in - to his eyes
Em7add4
Em7
and that is when I saw it...
C/E
Fadd9
Though he was still a - live...
Em/A
Am
he knew that he was dead...
f
71

G/A
Dm
To
see
a
ff
man
the
Em
mo
-
ment
when
he
Amsus4/2
Am7
Amsus4/2
dies...
Am7
Dm
I
see
that
look
a
-

Em7
E7sus4
gain
in
that
Am
man's
eyes!
rit.
sfz
fff
accel.
A5
sfz

Alone Here with You

Music and Lyrics by
Maury Yeston

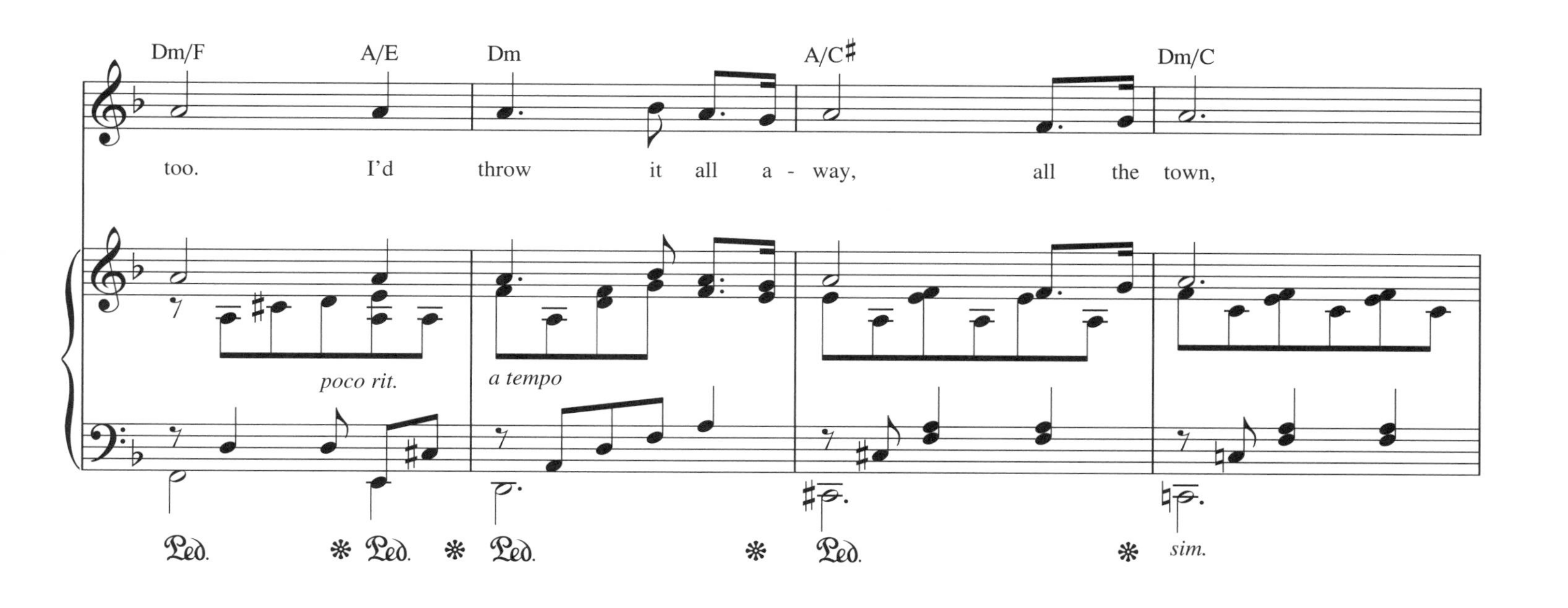
Dm/F
A/E
Dm
A/C♯
Dm/C
too. I'd throw it all a - way, all the town,
poco rit.
a tempo
sim.

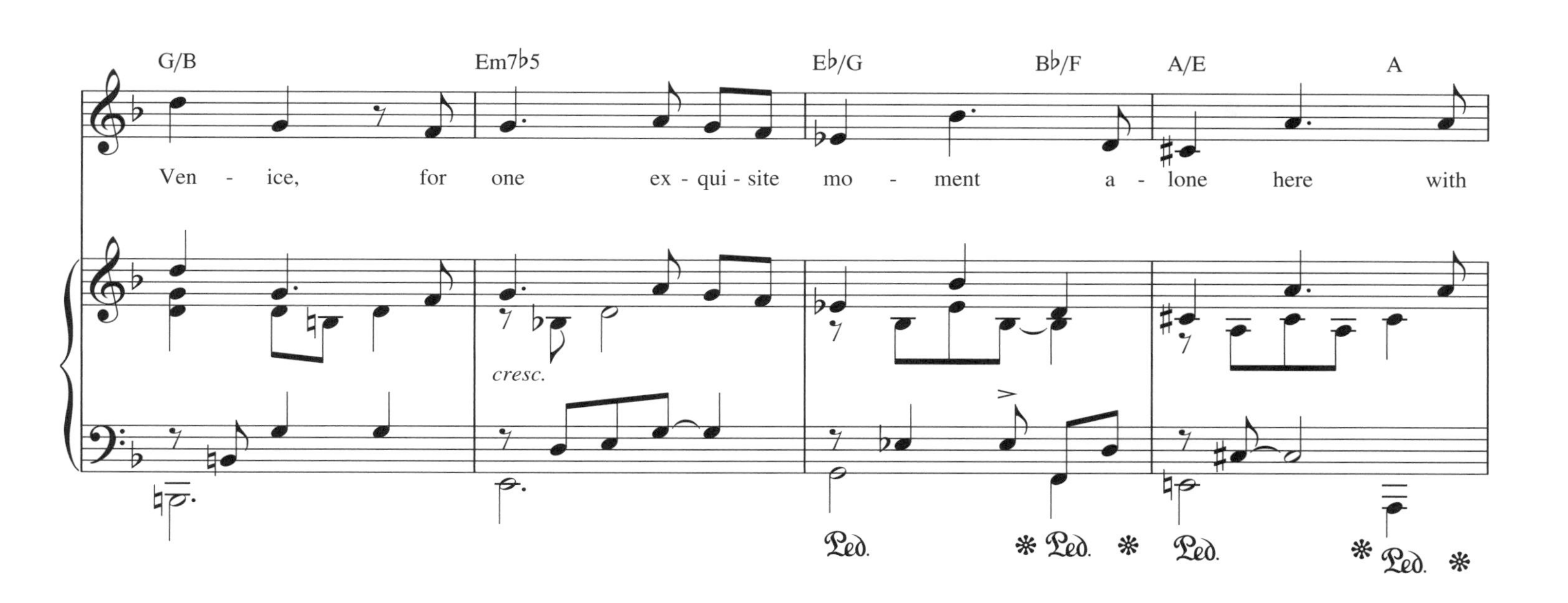
G/B
Em7♭5
E♭/G
B♭/F
A/E
A
Ven - ice, for one ex - qui - site mo - ment a - lone here with
cresc.

Slower
Dm
Gm/D
Dm
B♭
you. Give me love that grows and nev - er dies, one that
rit.
f
sim.

C9
F
B♭
Em7♭5
knows no com - pro - mise. One that keeps for - ev - er burn - ing, e -
E7
A
A(♭9)
E♭m
ter - nal - ly new. If the world could give to
mf poco rit.
a tempo
B♭/D
E♭m/D♭
A♭/C
F♭
me, as a crown, Ven - ice, and all that was with -
F♭/A♭
B♭
D°7/A♭
E♭m/G♭
D°7/F
E♭m
in it, each breath - tak - ing view, I'd cast it all a -
cresc.

B♭/D
E♭m/D♭
A♭/C
F♭
way all the town, Ven - ice, for one ex - qui - site
Ped.
sim.
F♭/A♭
C♭/G♭
B♭/F
B♭
E♭m
Em7♭5
mo - ment a - lone here with you.
sfz
Slower
Dm/A
Gm/A
Dm
B♭
Grazia: Give me love that grows and nev - er dies, all hel -
Sirki: Give me love that grows and nev - er dies, all hel -
ff molto rit.
sim.

C9
F
B♭
los and no good - byes. One that keeps for - ev - er
los and no good - byes. One that keeps for - ev - er
Em7♭5
E7
A
A(♭9)
burn - ing, e - ter - nal - ly new. If the
burn - ing, e - ter - nal - ly new.
rit.
E♭m
B♭/D
E♭m/D♭
A♭/C
world could give to me, as a crown, Ven - ice, and
If the world could give to me Ven - ice,
a tempo

F♭
F♭/A♭
B♭
D°7/A♭
E♭m/G♭
B♭/F
all that was with - in it, each breath - tak - ing view, I'd
and all with - in, each breath - tak - ing, breath - tak - ing
E♭m
B♭/D
E♭m/D♭
A♭/C
cast it all a - way, all the town, Ven - ice, for
view, cast it all a - way, Ven - ice, for
rit.
mp
sim.
Very slowly
F♭
F♭/A♭
C♭/G♭
B♭/F
B♭
Both: one ex - qui - site mo - ment a - lone here with
mp
rit.

E♭m
A♭m/E♭
B♭/E♭
you, a - lone with
f a tempo
mf
sim.
Ped.
G♭maj7
E♭m/G♭
C♭/E♭
you, to be
sfz
f
B♭/E♭
E♭
Fm7♭5/E♭
with you!
rit.
f a tempo
E♭
Fm7♭5/E♭
E♭
molto rit.

Losing Roberto

Music and Lyrics by
Maury Yeston

Slowly, with feeling ♩. = 46

N.C.

p

Ped. * *sim.*

pp

Am Dm6/A Am Fmaj9♯11/A

Stephanie: Los - ing Ro - ber - to, shot by a gun, when you

mf

8va

F Em7 Cadd9 F D9 F Fadd9

sev - er the bond 'twixt a moth - er and son... Once, my Ro - ber - to

8va

rit.

a tempo

G Am F/A C/E G
stood in that door, How I kissed him and missed him and sent him to
f
poco rit.
A Fmaj9♯11/A A Fmaj9♯11/A Cm Gm7
war. These were his sol - diers,
mp a tempo
mf
Cm Gm7 Cm F B♭ D G
that, his hat. Three win - ning chips from bac - ca - rat.
f
F/A F C D/F♯ Gm Em7♭5 Dm F G
Piled in that clos - et, toy up - on toy be - longed to Ro - ber - to, my

A G A
Gm7 C7sus4 C7
Fmaj7 B♭add9
boy. He sat at this win - dow, stared at that moon,
Em7♭5 A7
D A7/E D/F♯
Gm7 C7sus4 C7
wrote in his diary, dia - ry, played bas - soon. How he loved win - ter!
Fmaj7 B♭add9
Em7♭5 A7
Gm7 Am7 B♭
Hik - ing he'd go, leav - ing his foot - prints deep in the snow. They
poco rit.
Slower
Gm7 Am7
D C D
Slower
B♭ C
melt, but they're here with the rest. They melt, but not here in my

Tempo I
D C D
Am Dm6/A
Am Fmaj9♯11/A
breast.
No, my Ro - ber - to
will not de - part.
You can't
8va
mp
mf
F Em7 Cadd9 F D9
un - do a man, cut him free from your heart.
8va
Slower
F Fadd9 F G Am
Look! In that mir - ror,
comb - ing his hair,
no Ro -
Very slowly
F C G Em7
ber - to where once a Ro - ber - to was
mp
p

Tempo I
A5
Fmaj9♯11/A
A5
Fmaj9♯11/A
there.
a tempo
Quietly and reflectively
F
Fadd9
F
G
Am
Look! In that mir - ror,
comb - ing his hair,
no Ro -
Very slowly
F
C
G
Tacet
Tempo I
A5
Fmaj9♯11/A
ber - to where once a Ro - ber - to was there.
mp
A5
Fmaj9♯11/A
Am
mf

What Do You Do

Music and Lyrics by
Maury Yeston

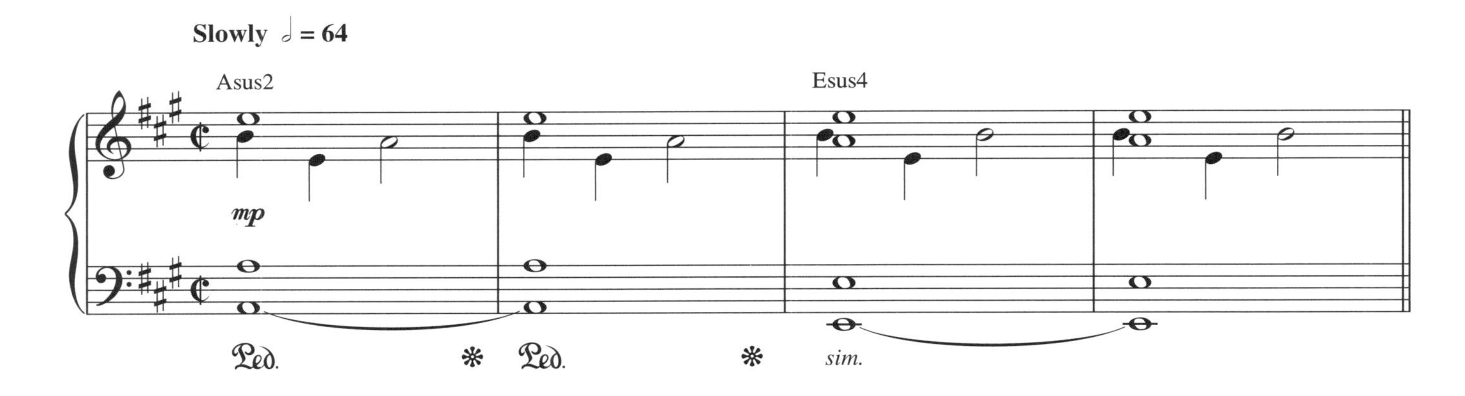

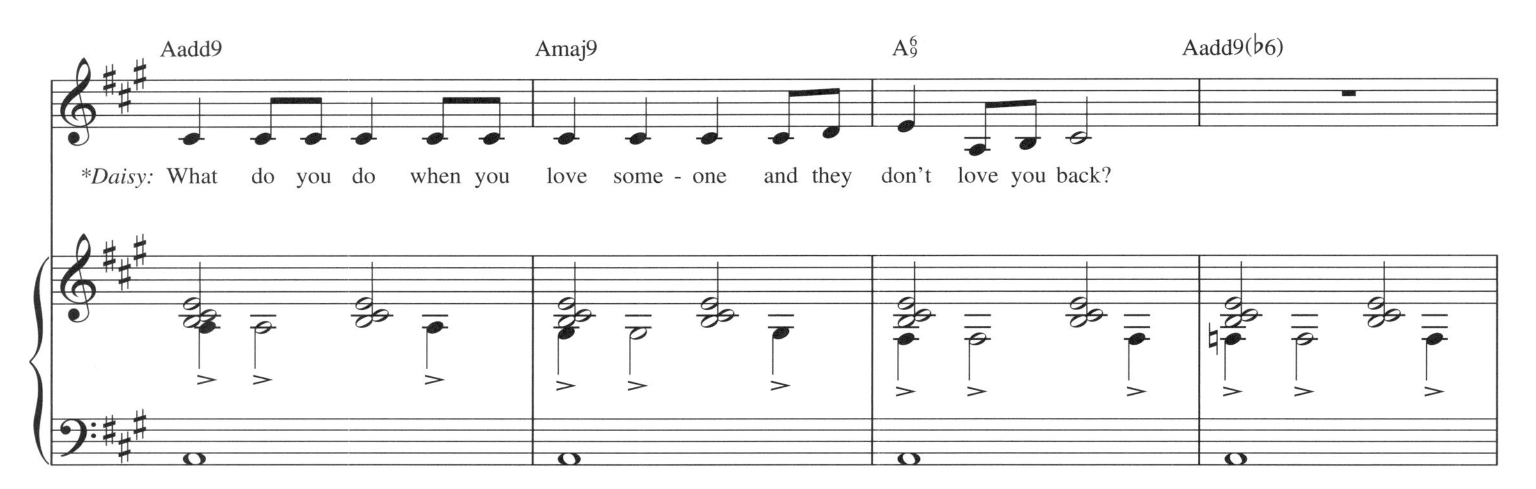

*Can be performed as a solo.

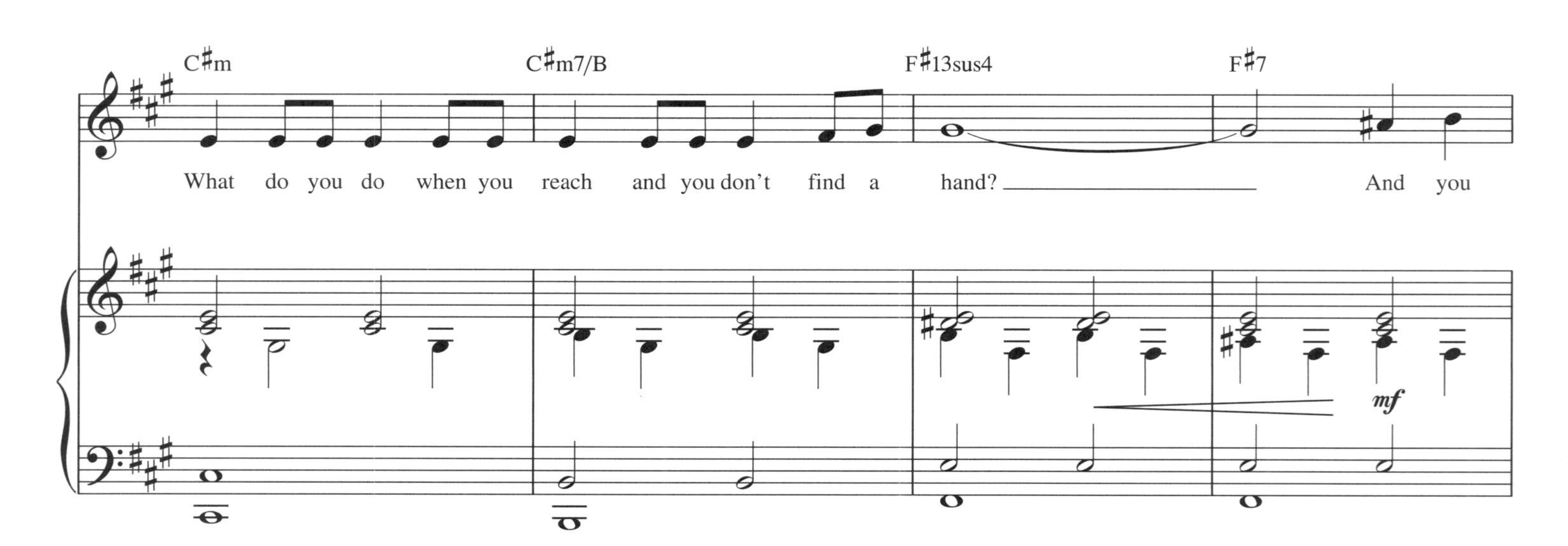

Badd9/F♯
Eadd9/F♯
Badd9/F♯
C♯7sus4
wait till it seems for - ev - er, and you hope that it can't be true. And
C♯add9/G♯
A♯m9
C♯/D♯
G♯7sus4
E7
if you can find a friend who'll un - der - stand, you're luck - y.
rit.
Aadd9
Aadd9/G♯
Aadd9/G
E/F♯
F♯7
What do you do when you give your heart till it aches with the pain?
mf a tempo
Bm
Bm/A
G♯/B♯
D♯°7
What if they don't hear your trum - pets and your drums? Oh, and
cresc.
sfz
f
poco rit.

Aadd9/E
E7sus4
Aadd9/E
B/D♯
that kind of love is blind - ing. It keeps you from ev - er find - ing you're
mf
a tempo
mp
Aadd9/E
Asus♯4/E
Dmaj7/E
E7sus4
E7
Aadd9
wait - ing for some - thing that nev - er comes.
D♭add9
D♭add9/C
D♭add9/C♭
B♭7♯5
B♭7
Corrado: What do you do when you give your heart till it aches with the pain?
f
E♭m
E♭m/D♭
C/E
G°7
What if they don't hear your trum - pets and your drums?
Both: Oh, and
cresc.
sfz
RH
ff

D♭add9/A♭
A♭7sus4
D♭add9
Gm7♭5
that kind of love is blind - ing. It keeps you from ev - er find - ing you're
D♭/A♭
G♭
D♭
E♭m7
D♭/F
G♭maj7
A♭7sus4
A♭7
A bit faster
D♭
wait - ing for some - thing that nev - er comes.
sfz
rit.
mf
G♭/D♭
G♭m/D♭
D♭
rit.

More and More

Music and Lyrics by
Maury Yeston

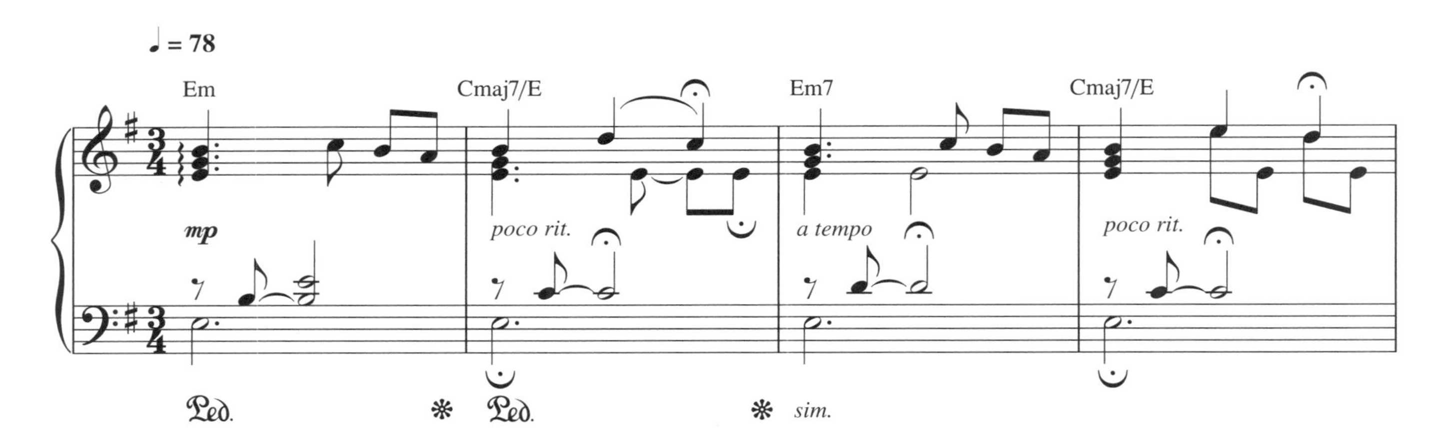

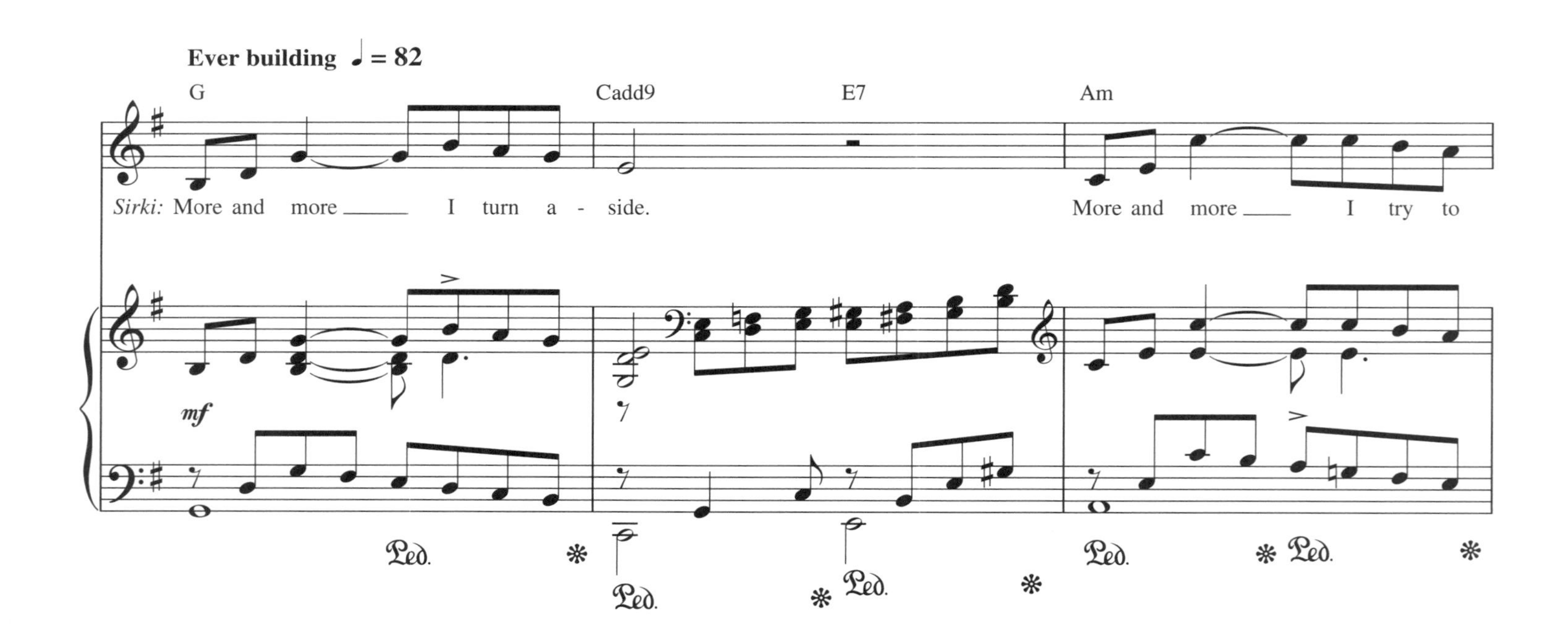

D9sus4 D7 D9sus4 D
hide my feel - ings.
G/B
More and more I try to
Cmaj7 C6 A/C♯
turn black white, and
G/D
make day night, and
D9sus4 D7 Cmaj7/D D7
fight my heart - beat.
Slower
G
More and more I can't go
Cadd9 E7
on.
Am
More and more I can - not
D9sus4 D7 D9sus4 D
be with - out you.
G/B
More and more I must be
Csus♯4/2 C Cmaj9 D♯°7
al - ways near you,
A bit slower
Em Cmaj7 D
not just one life - time,
poco rit.
a tempo
poco rit.
f
poco rit.
sim.
a tempo
più f

Gadd9/B Cmaj7 D Em C Gadd9/D Am7 Cmaj7/D D
not just one world a - lone. No, there will nev - er be e - nough; I will need you
sfz
G
Slower
B♭
E♭add9 G7
more! Grazia: All the more you turn a - way.
p
Cm
F9sus4 F7 F9sus4 F7 B♭/D
All the more you try to hide your se - cret. All the more you try to
E♭maj7 Cm/E♭ C/E B♭/F F9sus4 F7 E♭maj7/F F9
turn black white, and make day night, and fight my heart - beat.
rit.

G
Cadd9
E7
Am
Both: More and more I can't go on.
More and more I can - not
fff
rall.
a tempo

Cmaj7/D
D9
D9sus4
D7
G/B
C
Cmaj9
be with - out you.
More and more I must be al - ways near you,
più f

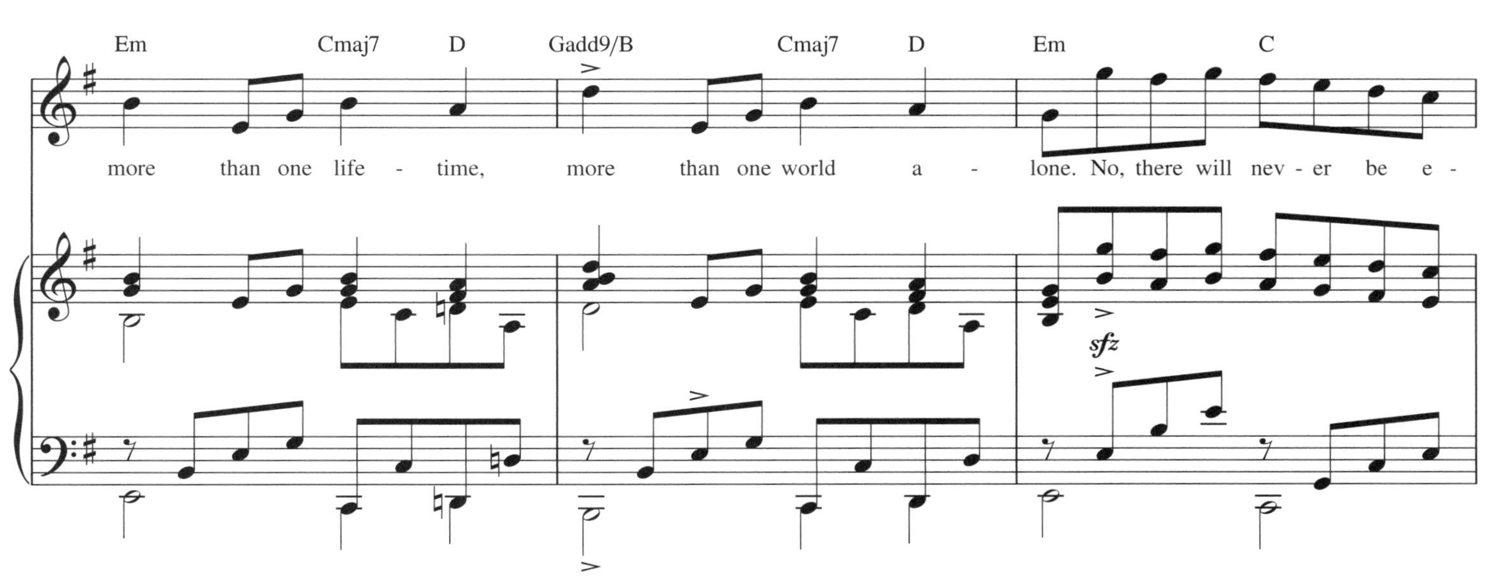
Em
Cmaj7
D
Gadd9/B
Cmaj7
D
Em
C
more than one life - time,
more than one world a - lone. No, there will nev - er be e -
sfz

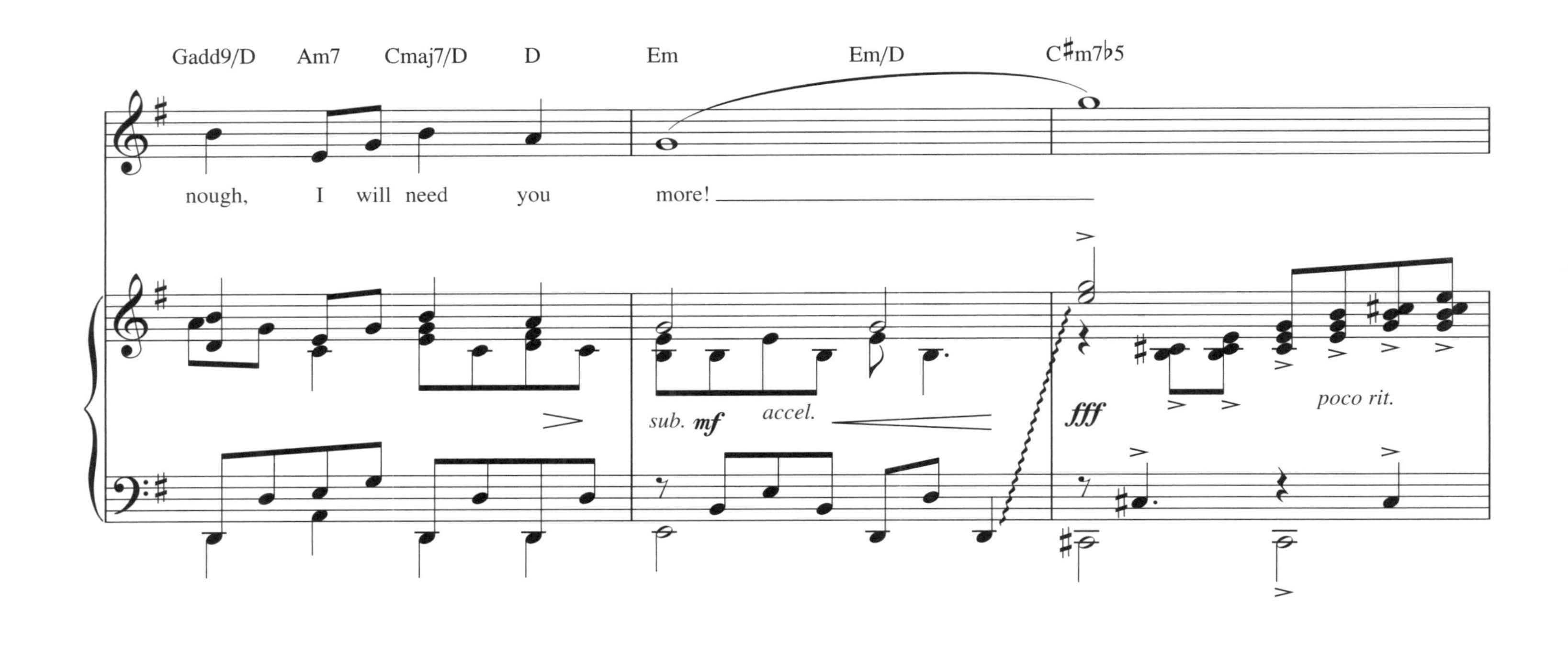
Gadd9/D Am7 Cmaj7/D D Em Em/D C♯m7♭5
nough, I will need you more!
sub. mf accel.
fff
poco rit.

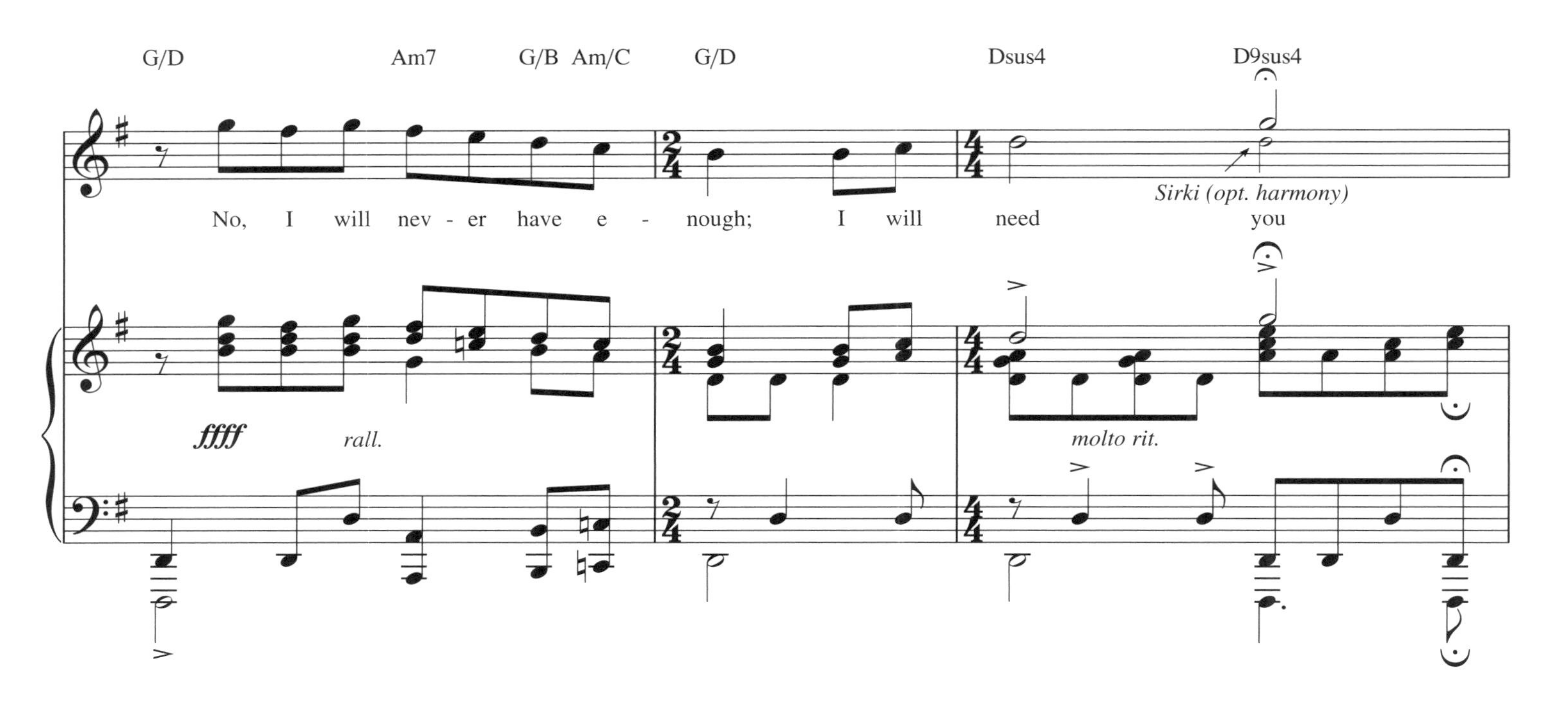
G/D Am7 G/B Am/C G/D Dsus4 D9sus4
No, I will nev - er have e - nough; I will need you
Sirki (opt. harmony)
ffff rall.
molto rit.

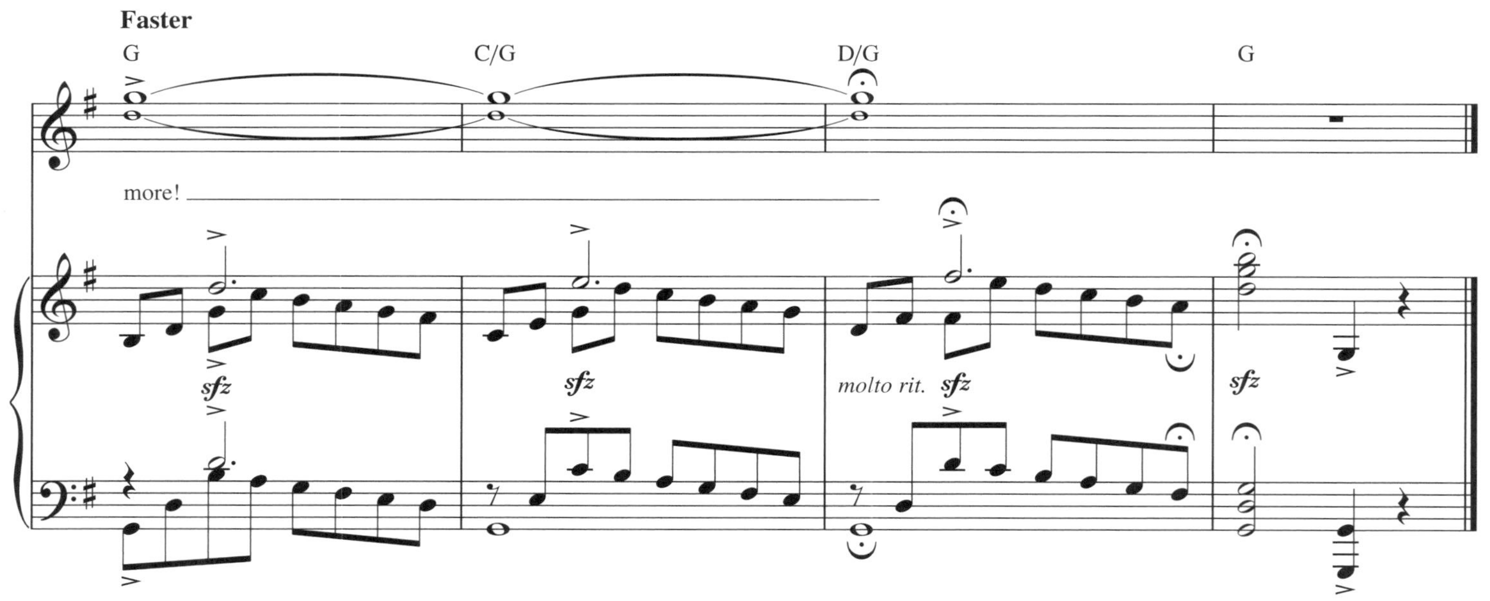
Faster
G C/G D/G G
more!
sfz
sfz
molto rit. sfz
sfz

Finally to Know

Music and Lyrics by
Maury Yeston

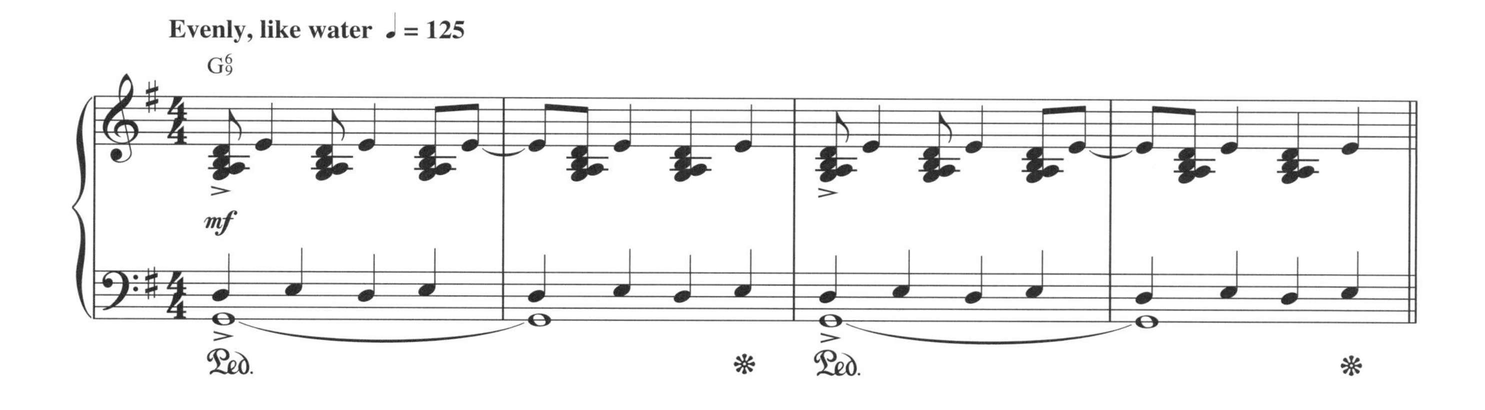

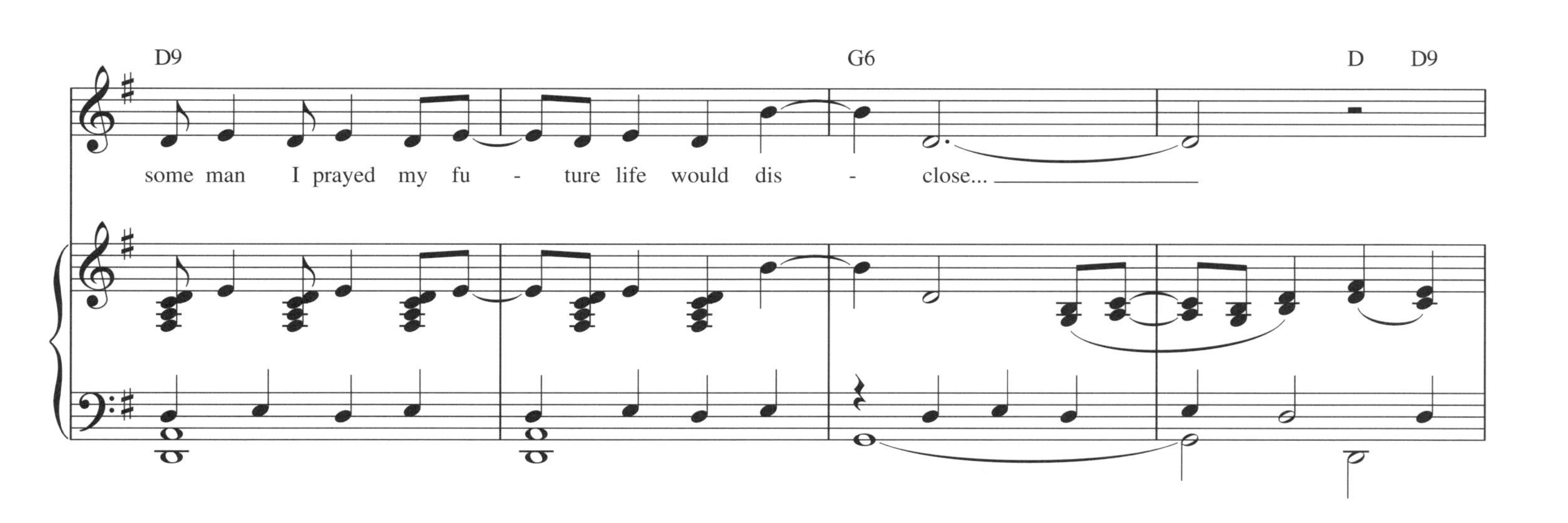

G6/9
D9sus4
Daisy: All of my life I'll wait for Cor-ra-do, know-ing that I'll come fol-low-ing af-ter,
D9
G
know-ing I'll go wher-ev-er Cor-ra-do goes...
G9sus4
C6/9
Alice: I thought my life was Gra-zi-a's broth-er. Some-how I know I must find an-oth-er
Cm6
G6/9/D
who makes me feel there could be no oth-er. And on the day I cap-ture that new love,

D9sus4
D9
G
D
D9
no long - er will I ev - er need to sup - pose...
G6/9
D9sus4
Grazia: You and me, we're
D9
Gadd9
D
D9
meant to be
Daisy: Cor - ra - do,
G6/9
D9sus4
Me and you, one

D9
G
house, one view.
G9sus4
G9
C6/9
Grazia, Alice, Daisy:
Make one heart, one
Cm6
G6/9/D
soul from two, from
D9
G
me and you...

G6/9
D9sus4
Grazia: Fi - n'lly now to know who I've wait - ed for,
Alice: Me and you, one
Daisy: All of my life I'll wait for Cor - ra - do, know-ing that I'll come fol - low-ing af - ter,
D9
G6/9
all these years I knew some - how he would come
house, one view.
hop-ing to go wher-ev - er Cor - ra - do goes.
G9sus4
C6/9
sweep in from a - far, take me in his arms.
Heart with heart, one
All of my life I've dreamed of Cor - ra - do, drawn to his side and lov - ing his laugh-ter,

Cm6
I have al - ways known
G6/9/D
he'd be there one day.
soul for two, that's
know-ing that I'll come fol - low-ing af - ter. Now I am sure I'll have my Cor - ra - do.
D9
He'd be there.
G
me and you.
No long - er will I ev - er need to sup - pose.
E♭
Grazia, Daisy:
A♭add♯4/2
A♭
Cm7/G
Alice:
No more to pine, no more to fret, no more to won - der now.

Fm
B♭7sus4 B♭7
E♭
I can be firm, de - ter - min - ing who he'll be.
C6
Fsus♯4/2
F
Am7/E
Clear as a bell, bright as the sun, sound - ing like thun - der now.
Dm7
Am7♭5
D7
There sim - ply can be on - ly one man be - side me...
sfz
G
C/G
D7/G
Grazia: Fi - n'lly to know!
Fi - n'lly to feel!
Alice, Daisy: Fi - n'lly to know!
Fi - n'lly to feel!

G9sus4
G7sus4
G7
Csus4
C
Noth - ing in doubt!
Be - liev - ing it's real!
Noth - ing in doubt!
Be - liev - ing it's real!

A/C♯
C♯°7
G/D
All my life spent in wish - ing it so,
All my life spent in wish - ing it so,
rit. poco a poco

A9sus4
A7
D9sus4
D7
All: fi - n'lly to know my one true...
rit.

Slower
Alice: G
D7/G
Daisy: Fi-n'lly to know, fi-n'lly to know, fi-n'lly my one true love...
mp
A/C♯
G/D
Slower
A9sus4
Grazia: All my life spent in wish-ing it so... Fi-n'lly to know
mp
rit.
p
mf
A7
D9sus4
D7
Very slow
Alice: G
my one true...
Daisy: Fi-n'lly to know, fi-n'lly to know, fi-n'lly my
rit.
mp
E♭maj7♯5/G
Faster
G
one true
Grazia, Alice, Daisy: love...
8va
sfz
sfz
rit.
Ped.
*

I Thought That I Could Live

Music and Lyrics by
Maury Yeston

In 2 𝅗𝅥 = 102
F♯m7♭5
B7sus♯4
B7sus4
B7
Em
Am/E
awe-some spec-ter all men dread...
Hold-ing me here...
rit.
mf
Em7
Am
Em
Am6/E
this in-ex-'ra-ble force with the pow'r to cre-ate a new
sim.
Em
D7/E
Em7
A/E
life draws you in!
This re-mark-a-ble gran-
sfz
f
rit.
C/E
F♯/E
Am/E
deur that fills you with won-der-ment, love draws you
rit.
ff
sfz
a tempo
mf

Am7♭5/E♭
Em
C
in
with its light...
rit.
In 4 ♩ = 106
C7
F
At least I got to live be-neath the sun to
poco rit.
mf
Dm
B♭maj7
know of pow-ers I've not un-der-stood, to learn how pre-cious life may be and
B♭/C
Dm
C/E
F
un-der-stand the pain of ev-er leav - ing... to learn it is a res-er-voir of
f

Dm
light, and feel a love that roots me to this place. Who -
B♭maj7 Gm7 C7sus4 Dm
ev - er could have dreamed it would be life I'd be most grate - ful for re - ceiv -
C/E B♭ C Dm C7/E Fsus4 F
ing? The gift to learn the depth of hu - man feel - ing,
want - ed so to know this love men cling to,
B♭ C Dm C7/E F
and come to know life's pow - er to en - thrall,
what makes them fight and hold on fast through all.

Dm G Am G7/B
and see the world a - new from men's per -
And so I found, like them, a girl to

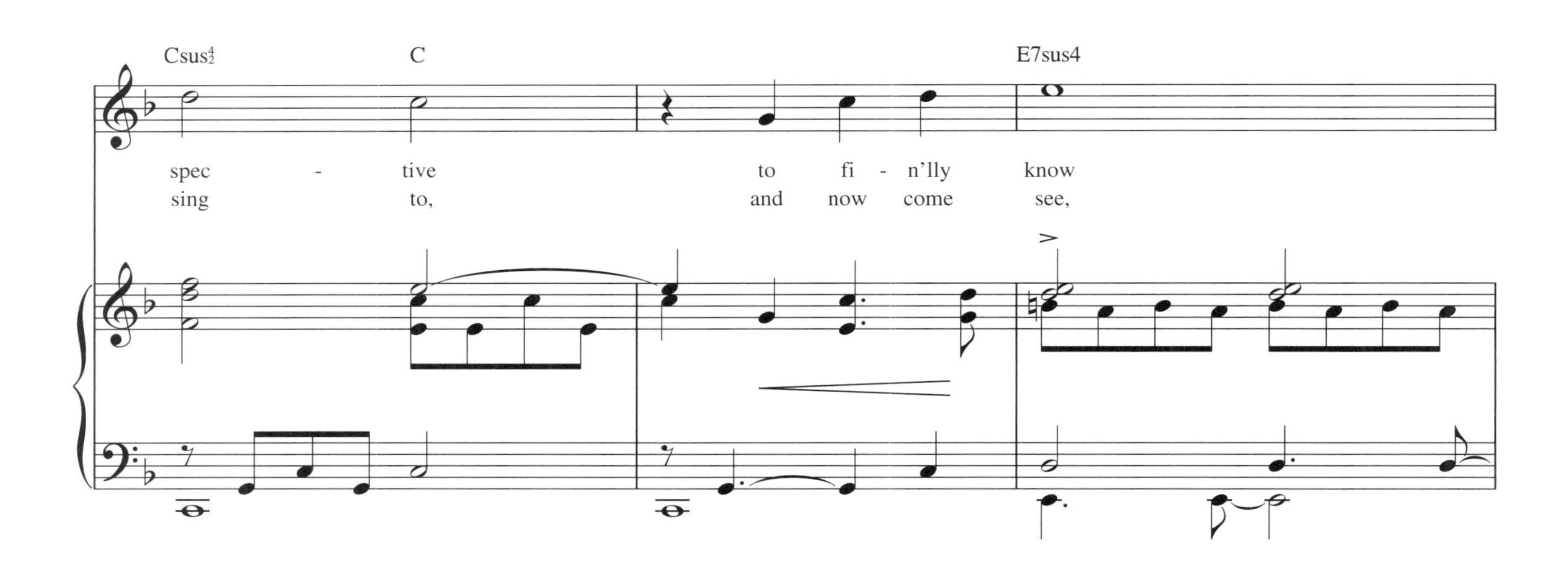
Csus$^4_2$ C E7sus4
spec - tive to fi - n'lly know
sing to, and now come see,

C9
why men fall and call:
as I fall, I cry:

In 2 𝅗𝅥 = 102
To Coda
F
E♭6/9
B♭
C
"Dear God, mer - cy on our
"Dear God, take me now in -
fff
Dm
C/E
poor souls!
F
E♭6/9
Dear God,
B♭
C
Dm
take us not a - way

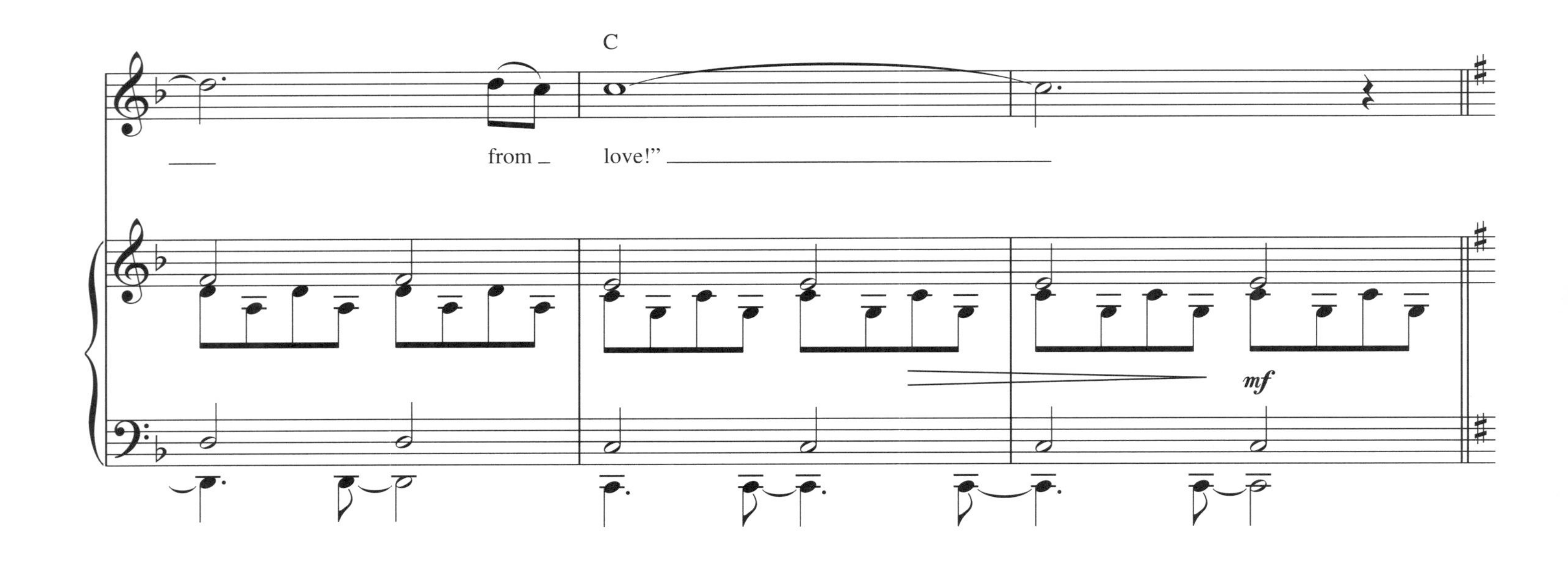
C
from love!"
mf

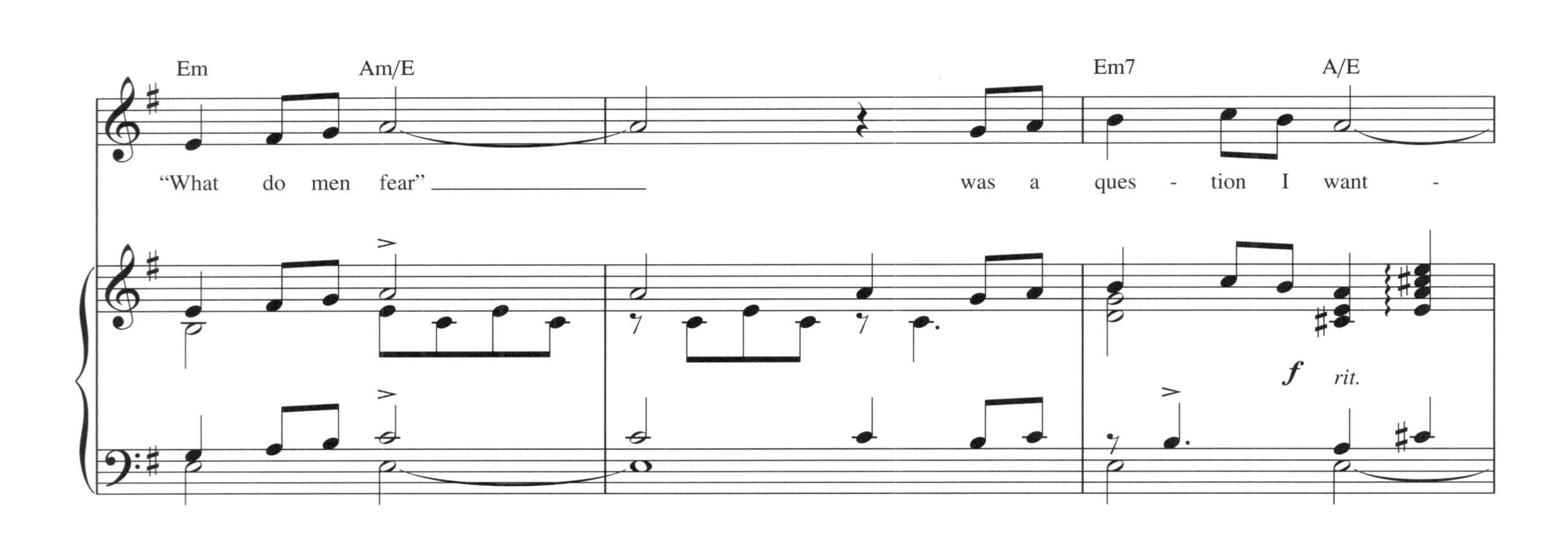
Em
Am/E
Em7
A/E
"What do men fear"
was a ques - tion I want -
f
rit.

C/E
F♯/E
Am/E
ed to an - swer, and now
I'm like them: what I
rit.
ff
sfz
a tempo
mf

Am7♭5/E♭
Em
C
fear
is my - self...
rit.
a tempo
In 4 ♩ = 106
C7
F
I've
come to know the na - ture of the world,
and
poco rit.
mf
Dm
B♭maj7
how can I now ex - it as I came?
No, how can I de - stroy the ver - y
Gm7
C7sus4
Dm
C/E
D.S. al Coda
beau - ty and the glo - ry I've been find - ing?
I

Coda
Dm
C/E
F
stead
of
her
E♭6/9
B♭
C
and
give
life
to
the
Tacet B♭maj9/D
Tacet B♭maj7♭5/D
one
I
ffff
C
C+
C
love!"
sffz

December Time

Music and Lyrics by
Maury Yeston

Am7
your heart may lose its way.
D9 Am7 C/D
Un - til you reach De - cem - ber time,
Am7 D9 Gadd9
hap - py end - ing? Who can say?
Gadd9
Your life flies by in pan - to - mime,

Am7♭5/G
Gadd9
but words re - quire some de - lay...
Ped.
C/D
All good po - et - ry takes time.
You don't hear the fi - nal
Gadd9/D
Cm/D
D7
G
rhyme un - til you reach De - cem - ber time.
rit.
a tempo
G7
C/G
Think of the sweet grapes on the vine.
When they're com -

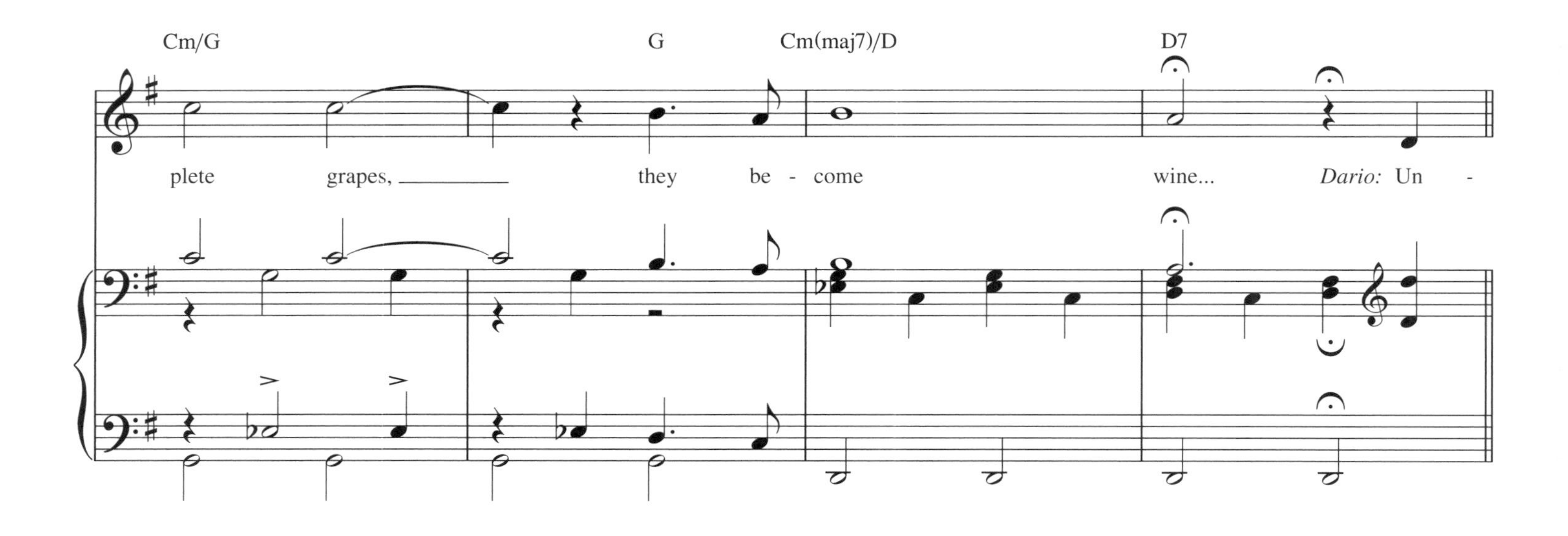
Cm/G
G
Cm(maj7)/D
D7
plete grapes, they be - come wine... Dario: Un -

Gadd9
Evangelina: De - cem - ber time,
Dario: til you reach De - cem - ber time, your
Ped.
sim.

Am7
D9
your heart may lose, may lose its way. Un -
heart may lose its way. Un -

Am7
C/D
Both: til you reach De - cem - ber time, happy - py
Am7
D9
Gadd9
Gadd9
end - ing? Who can say? Evangelina: Your life flies
sfz
G
Gadd9
Am7♭5/G
by well past its prime. So quick, it seems but a
rit.
Slower
G
C/D
day... Both: All good po - et - ry takes time. You don't hear the fi - nal

Gadd9/D
Am7♭5/D
D7
G
rhyme until you reach De - cem - ber time.
G7
C/G
Evangelina:
Dario:
Think of the sweet grapes on the vine.
Am7♭5/G
G
D7/G
Slowly
Gadd9
When they're com - plete grapes, drink the wine!
Ped.
G

Pavane

Music and Lyrics by
Maury Yeston

F/C
G/B
E♭/B♭
born, some may die, a pa - vane. We dance
A7
Dm
on as we learn.
mp
Ped.
B7 Aadd9/C♯ B/D♯
Em
All: Sea - sons come, sea - sons
sim.
B/D♯
G/D
A/C♯
go, first the leaves, then the snow, then the
mf cresc.

F/C
B7
Em/G
B/F♯
rain and the sun will re - turn.
On the
f
mf
Em
B/D♯
G/D
earth, in the sky, some are born, some may
A/C♯
F/A
B7
die, a pa - vane. We dance on as we
3
poco rit.
Em
learn.
a tempo
rit.
Ped.
*
Ped.
*
Ped.
*

Bathing Music

Music by
Maury Yeston

L.H.
R.H.
Ped.
f
sim.
8va
sfz
mp
sub. mp
accel. poco a poco
rit.
mf